RECONNECT WITH LOVE

A Spiritual Guide to Building Supernatural Mental Health and Relationships

Mac McMillan

Reconnect with Love

ISBN 978-0-9812894-1-0
e-book ISBN 978-0-9812894-0-3

Printed and bound in the United States of America.

Published by Dean McMillan in 2023.

I dedicate this book to my parents, who introduced me to Love at a young age.

This Book Is for You...

If you've been wandering through life without knowing and experiencing Love...

If you've spent any part of life unaware of how valuable and loveable you are...

If you don't yet know what your purpose in life is, or how to achieve it...

If you've connected with Love in your past, but not experienced Love daily...

If you try to love in your own strength but don't feel empowered by Love...

If you have more struggles, confusion, chaos, and strife than Love...

If Fear, Shame, and Pride have influenced you more than Love...

Table of Contents

z

An Introduction

I know you've heard of me. You've also felt me at times. I made sure of it. But there were times when I was there you didn't notice, and I wanted you to. When you were made fun of and mocked, I was there. When you were discouraged and crying, I was there. When you were beaten and bruised outside and inside, I was with you.

I was with you through the triumphs of your life, and the failures. When you've hurt others, I never left you. When my enemies attacked you, I had your back, and your front. I have never given up on you. I've never turned my back on you. I was there when you needed me most. I stayed when others left. Sure, you could have helped yourself. That's how I made you. But I wanted to go with you on your journey. I wanted to cheer you on, champion your cause, and hold the trophies with you.

I wanted you to wake up with me in your mind. I'm thrilled when you think of me during the day. I never stop thinking of you. You are the apple of my eye and the jewel of my crown. There's never a time when I stop bragging about you. You make my heart want to sing, and I do...I sing about you all the time.

Sometimes I let you feel my absence, but it's only so you long for me more and realize how much you need me. I never really go anywhere because I'm everywhere and somewhere all at once. You're safe wherever you go and whatever you experience because I'm with you. There's no danger with me. I have no opposition that is my equal.

I want to create in you and with you. I want to build beautiful strong towers in your mind that you can take shelter in when storms surge. I want you to look out from atop those towers with peace in your heart, knowing nothing can change how valuable and lovable you are. I want the assurances I give you every day to melt your heart so I can flow in and out of you.

You'll be amazed at what we can do when you truly know and experience me. I have plans for us. Those plans are the outworking of my heart for you. Take care of our time together. Treasure it as I do. When we're together, I'll inspire you. When you're listening to me, I'll give you truth nuggets to chew on that will feed your soul.

You'll want me like I want you. And if you want me, you'll get me. I have everything you want and need. If you have me...you have everything!

I see you...I love you...Come find me.

Love

SECTION ONE: The Who and What of Love

Chapter 1: The Nature of Love

Have you ever had to prove your love to someone? If so, how did you do it? I bet it wasn't just with words, right? No, to prove love you must have actions. Were the actions you used to prove your love about what *you* wanted, needed, or liked? If that was the case, you probably failed to prove your love. To prove love, actions must be about what the *other* person wants, needs, or likes. We know love is others-centred, but what else do we know about Love?

We know Love is kind, caring, tender, and compassionate. Love is gentle, warm, and inviting. Love is thoughtful and empathetic. Love is truthful; it never lies nor deceives, and it's always open and real. Love is hopeful and faithful. Love is passionate, friendly, and unconditional. Love is also selfless, patient, and sacrificial in nature. Love too is wise and instructional. Love protects and provides. And Love gives choices—it promotes freedom and goodness. Love inspires and teaches. Love encourages and gives freely. Love is also mysterious and joyful. I could go on and on I'm sure, and only scratch the surface of what Love truly is.

What if Love was also a relational spiritual *Being* that knew everything, could do anything good, and owned everything? Imagine if that Spirit wanted to be your friend—wanted to hang out with you all the time. What if that Being that IS Love was your greatest cheerleader, most trusted confidant, and just thought the world of you?

That would mean, from the moment you wake up every morning, to the moment you go to sleep, and even while you slumber—the one who IS Love is out for your good. Think of that Love Being as a relationship (that identifies as they, them, we) that is energized and activated to protect you, provide for you, encourage you, lead and teach you, gently correct you, and guide you to people and circumstances that make your life the best it can possibly be. What if that Spirit, who IS Love, would sacrifice anything to help you?

If you think about it, someone who doesn't HAVE Love, but IS Love, cannot *not* love you! That would mean, no matter what you do or don't do, say or don't say, Love can't withhold love from you based on their mood, opinion or whim. That would also mean you could do nothing to be more or less loved by Love. For Love to love is not a choice—it's just the nature of Love to love. Love doesn't rely on your behaviour, attitudes, opinions, or beliefs to determine the amount of love to give. You would get all of Love every day, no matter what.

Wouldn't you want to hang out with such a Being? Wouldn't you want them in your corner all the time? No one would ever say, "Nah, I don't need more Love in my life" or "Don't you push Love on me." That would be ridiculous, wouldn't it?

Now, what if that Love-Being also designed you—what if you were Love's child? What if they thought you up, made you and wanted you to be just the way you are? What if Love gave you all your capabilities for good, and then made it so you'd have plenty of opportunities to practice those capabilities with the rest of their children? What if you could participate in Love's joy of giving?

What if Love fashioned you like a funnel that Love could flow through—not a pitcher that just pours out, nor a cup that just receives—but a vessel through which Love flows in and out? What if that flow involved experiencing crazy amounts of joy, hope, peace, contentment, fulfillment, and excitement every day of your life? You might even describe that as heaven on earth, don't you think? But what if Love designed it so that you could only experience the flow coming in and going out to the degree you are *CONNECTED* to the source—the one who IS Love?

My dad used to tell me, "Show me your friends and I'll tell you who you are." I didn't like that lesson because I knew it was a shot at my friends and the kind of person I was becoming. I didn't like it because it was true. I found out later it was in the Bible—in Proverbs somewhere—but I didn't look it up because I didn't want to give my dad the benefit of the dig. The thinking is that whoever we hang out with the most is who we become like. So, if there is a Being who IS Love, and we're hanging out with them all the time, that would mean Love would rub off on us and it would be obvious to everyone. Everyone would want to know us and be around us in hopes they could become like us.

If you said, "I'm a close friend of Justin Bieber" or "I know Tiger Woods personally" or "King Charles texts me every day," it's more than likely someone would reply, "Oh yeah? Prove it!" The reason you'd be asked to prove those claims is because the person you're talking to esteems that celebrity and if you were a friend of theirs that would be impressive. That person would probably start esteeming you and want to hang out. The thinking is, if that celebrity wants to hang out with this person in front of me, they must be cool. There must be something awesome about them. And they might think, "If I hang out with this person, maybe I could meet that celebrity. Maybe the celebrity would think I'm cool and want to hang out with me too."

How would you prove you knew a celebrity...if they weren't into taking selfies with you, that is? You could show gifts that have the celebrity's signature on them, I suppose. But really, you could get gifts from anyone, or buy them yourself, and you could forge a signature. If you suddenly became richer, like a celebrity, that might impress someone. But you could get wealth on your own in another way too. You could start talking and acting like a celebrity. You could wax eloquently about all the personal facts and family history you know about that celebrity. You could even get together with a host of celebrity impersonators and form clubs. But in the end, that's just mimicry, memorization, and odd gatherings that anyone could do, and it's really not that impressive.

The most foolproof way to prove you know someone is to show up at your friend's door with the celebrity beside you. If a celebrity shows up with their arm around you and goes on and on about how much they adore you and can't get enough of you, that would be a ringing endorsement and absolute proof that you are close friends. That would be impressive and likely garner you favour with everyone you know. Everyone would want what you have—a close friendship with someone they look up to.

If we're best friends with Love, and maybe even have the Spirit of Love in our hearts, then everyone would see proof, because Love rubbing off on us would make us very impressive in our actions and attitudes. In that case, everyone would want to know and hang out with Love like we get to. Everyone would be asking us to *CONNECT* them with Love too.

But what if Love has enemies out to destroy their design and offspring? Wouldn't it make sense that such enemies would be invested in *DISCONNECTING* us from the source that is Love? What if the enemies' aim is to do that by clouding our awareness of who Love is, who we are, and why we're here? If the enemies could accomplish that they would disrupt the flow of Love, which would make life unfulfilling or miserable for those whose sole purpose it is to have Love flow in and out of them.

If that were the case, it would be vital to figure out how to defeat those enemies and *RECONNECT* with the one who IS Love. That's what my work, and this book, are all about. I consider Love as such a Being—a Spirit-Relationship if you will—who IS Love—and ourselves as their creation.

I believe the consequences of disconnecting from Love are a confused and troubled mind, a guarded or wounded heart, and unfulfilling or broken relationships. These states of mind and heart can lead to the presence of anxiety, depression, and addictions. I believe disconnection from Love equates to the loss of true freedom. And I want to help people be set free to know true Love.

No doubt you've heard the phrase, "The truth will set you free." But have you ever asked yourself: free *from* what? And free *to* what? And what is *free*, anyway? For that matter, what is *Truth?* Well, if what I just described to you is the true nature of reality, then knowing who Love is, living with the knowledge of how valuable and loveable we are, and fulfilling the purposes for which Love designed us, is the ultimate Freedom. The truth, then, sets us free to walk in awareness of the realities of Love. In short, maybe freedom in life is knowing who Love is, who we really are, and why we're here. And, perhaps for freedom to exist, we need to move away from the enemies of Love and their influence over our awareness and practice of our design. To do that...maybe we need to be *RECONNECTED WITH LOVE!*

It's easy to see that we've all become disconnected with the one who is Love. Love is about relationship and relationship is at the root of every problem in the world right now. Just turn to any news app on your phone and you'll see many problems that boil down to a lack of Love in relationships. Mental health, addictions, and family counsellors are so busy. There's a waitlist for most of them and treatment centres are usually full. Though there are numerous factors in such problems, relationship is always part of the root issue. Relationship only becomes problematic when there's a lack of Love. So, *Reconnecting with Love* is the start to fixing most problems in society. It's also the beginning of *Building Supernatural Mental Health and Relationships!*

Two Connections

There are two types of *Reconnections with Love*. One is a big connection. It is a *Life Reconnection*. That type requires *surrender* and *commitment*. It's not an act of the mind, but of the *heart,* because it involves ultimate *trust* and *faith* in the one who IS Love. That is a one-time decision that reverberates through an entire lifetime.

The second type of *Reconnection with Love* is a smaller but crucial practice. That requires *turning our attention* towards Love on a daily basis. This is a decision of the *mind* to tune out any messages of the *enemies*, that could come from sources of influence, such as Hollywood, or social media, or news media.

Some people attempt to skip the big *Reconnection with Love,* because they're not into surrendering to anyone, and they're not ready to fully trust. So, they just turn their attention to Love in as many daily moments as they can remember to. Their attempts at small *Reconnection* never last nor have much impact, because they're not plugged in to the power source—Love.

Other people do the big reconnection with Love, but then for many reasons don't do the daily reconnections. Perhaps it's the busy lifestyles they lead. Or it may be the big reconnection with Love didn't really do for them all they hoped it would, so they slowly tune out Love and stay that way until a crisis hits.

The problem with that approach is, if I ignore you, I'm not likely to hear you. If I pay attention to you, I'm more likely to hear you, right? Basic common sense really. For years I ignored the Spirit of Love in me and paid more attention to the world around me. It's easy to do. Watching sports, TV, movies, news media, social media, the music industry, substance use, and sex are all entertaining distractions from life's stresses and busy schedules. That's why, after doing a big reconnection with Love as a young man, my mental health and relational health became worse off than before I surrendered. I wasn't doing the daily Reconnection with Love.

An old saying goes, "Delight yourself in the one who IS Love and they will give you the desires of your heart." I take that to mean if we go to the Spirit of Love for our sense of pleasure and stress relief, they give us a greater sense of their presence and desired purpose. That's what we long for if we're filled with the Spirit of Love—to be more aware of Love's presence and purpose. That's true freedom, and it leads to supernatural mental and relational health, as well as powerful influence for Love. Just think of Mother Teresa of Calcutta. Now that was a woman who knew and heard from the one who IS Love, and her legacy of love lives on today.

We can't all be like Mother Teresa, but we can all make a difference in our families and communities. But to have positive influence, experience true contentment of freedom, and to be our authentic selves, we must learn how to reconnect with Love.

Let me make this perfectly clear from the outset: supernatural mental health and relationships require *both* forms of Reconnection with Love. If you're happy with a "just good enough" state of mental health and relationship strength this world has to offer, there are plenty of other resources to facilitate that. But if you want supernatural mental health and relationships, then you must find your way to life reconnection and daily reconnection with the one who is Love.

By "supernatural" I mean beyond what our natural minds can comprehend. By supernatural mental health I mean beyond what our human knowledge and skill can build. By supernatural relationships I mean beyond what two people can construct on their own. Love, the Being, is supernatural. Whatever Love does is supernatural. Whatever supernatural Love builds has the strength to last forever. But Love does need partners for maintenance of what they build. That's where we come in.

Our Part:

Some time ago I sat down and wrote out all that I knew about Love. I wrote all the qualities and characteristics of Love that have been revealed throughout human history and in my own life. Then I pictured these qualities as a person—Love personified. I didn't fashion a higher power in my image. I just wrote out what that higher power revealed to me through history and life.

Every day I now have conversations with the one who IS Love. I invite Love to teach me, bless me, correct me, change me, and, most of all, to give me a heightened awareness of their presence. I decided to go to Love for all my entertainment. All my leisure time is dedicated to Love.

Since I started searching and hearing, Love has helped me heal old wounds and restore relationships. Love has helped me overcome addiction. Love has helped me encourage and inspire thousands of people to heal, learn and grow in their relationships, minds, and spirits. Love has restored my faith and given me hope, joy and priceless contentment. With Love I've been enjoying the ride of my life, and you can too!

Why not ask Love to do the same for you? Ask the one who IS Love to lead you to the Truth about Love, your value and incredible purpose. Then keep the eyes and ears of your heart and mind open to perceiving from Love. Look for Love's messages that will often come through people and circumstances. Love wants you to search and is eager to be found by each and everyone of us. Love wants us all to hear the Truth that can build *Supernatural Mental Health and Relationships*. But first we must discover how to *Reconnect with Love*.

Chapter 2: A Personal Story of Reconnection

I grew up in a pastor's home. They say preacher's kids are either the best in the church or the worst. I was not the best. But I did a heartfelt *Reconnection with Love* by *surrendering* and *committing* my life to Love early on. Well, as heartfelt as you can muster as a snot-nosed kid. From that moment on, I felt different. Even as a kid, when I was walking along the sidewalk by myself, I could hear Love's voice inside me, and I knew it was different than my own voice. I believe that children have better spiritual intuition. Maybe that's because there's less to cloud their spiritual senses.

But for the most part, I was just a normal kid. Life happened. I got distracted from Love by sports and girls, as many teenage boys do. At one point I made another big *Reconnection with Love* after being disillusioned by fickle friends and the party scene. In that moment of returning, I clearly heard Love say to my mind, "I never left you." And from that moment on I never needed another big *Reconnection with Love*. I was hooked on Love.

In my late teens I travelled around the world with some friends of my family who were going around helping people. I got to see Love in action in powerful ways I'd never witnessed before. There was a boy who'd never walked without braces on his legs. After we asked Love to heal him, the boy took off the braces and ran around. There were blind people who could suddenly see. There were people having seizures that were suddenly calmed. All kinds of other miracles took place right in front of our eyes that we couldn't explain with our natural minds. My commitment to Love was validated and solidified.

The problem was I was still affected by *the enemies of Love,* and I thought my big *Reconnection with Love* would just take care of the *enemies*. It didn't. Later in life, *Fear, Shame*, and *Arrogance* started wreaking havoc with my marriage, family life, and vocation. I was living a double life. To the outside world I seemed a model husband, father, and leader in the community. On the inside I was addicted to *Lust*.

Lust was my coping strategy for any emotional pain. The *enemies* were flashing thoughts that led to feelings I didn't want. To get rid of those emotions I would fantasize, fulfill sexual desires in a way that contradicted my conscience and integrity, not to mention the expectations and standards of others. And then I was right back to *Shame* feelings and *Fear* thoughts. It destroyed my marriage, family life, and career.

Over the ensuing years, Love would intervene and give me realizations that helped my battles with the *enemies*. Love was kind enough to use my pain and triumphs to help other people through addictive thinking and behaviour. Yet the war was always going on inside me to some degree. Thankfully, I didn't have to be perfect for Love to bless me or use me for supernatural purposes.

Lately, Spirit started doing something in my life that has led to complete freedom from addictive thinking and behaviour. Spirit changed my desires, supernaturally charged my *Mental Health*, and restored and revitalized my *Relationships*. I don't know why it happened now. Who can understand the timing of Love? All I know is I've become a completely different person inside and I believe it's starting to show on the outside.

Chapter 3: The Resources of Love

Where do we start with this *Reconnection with Love*? Perhaps we should start by describing what our Spirit-Parent has to offer. Coincidentally, it's the exact ingredients we humans need. So, as we look at the needs every human has, think of them also as the riches that Love has and wants to offer each of us.

The soul was built a bit like the body, in that it has three basic needs it cannot live without: air, food, and water. If it doesn't receive these needs from healthy sources, it will go looking to unhealthy sources, or at least try to distract itself from the fact that it's suffocating, starving, or dehydrated.

Air to the soul is called *Security*, which refers to feeling safe in every way we can, and valuable for who we are. Food for the soul is called *Significance*, which refers to the abilities and insights we have to offer the world. And water for the soul is called *Service*, which refers to the motivational gifts that compel us to help those for whom we feel compassion. Since Love desires to give us all these needs, we should understand each of them more thoroughly.

SECURITY – Soul Air

By *security* I mean to feel *safe*—physically, emotionally, socially, mentally, and spiritually—and *valuable* for who we are. Every human needs to feel safe and valued for who they are, and this is self-evident. Let's think of security like a cake, with several ingredients that make up security. And so that it's relatable for all of us, let's put it in the context of a child growing up. The question is, "What do children need in order to feel physically, emotionally, mentally, socially, and spiritually safe and valued for who they are?" In this list we may just find the air Love has, and wants, to breathe into our souls.

Provision – Every child needs a roof over their head, clothes on their back and food in their belly. They also need a space to call their own. Such things are just basic to feeling safe.

Protection – Every child needs to be protected from physical, mental, emotional, and sexual harm that may come from both outside and inside the family.

Parents – I believe single parents can give security. However, when parents split up in front of their children, that can introduce some insecurity. A child might start wondering, "Jeez, who else is going to leave me? Maybe I'm not important enough to stick around for or pursue a relationship with." But just because parents stay together doesn't guarantee they are giving security either. They must have a type of relationship and home life for it to lead to security.

Stability – A child can't be constantly worried that mom and dad are going to split up. They need to live in the assurance that their parents' relationship is solid. For security to exist, the thought of their parents splitting up can't even be in the mind of the child.

Consistency – A child can't be walking on eggshells around the house wondering the next time mom and dad are going to "lose it" on each other. The child must know that the good they expect to happen from their parents almost always occurs.

Kind Communication – For a child to know they are valuable they need to be spoken to with warmth. If there's a lot of yelling and screaming, or silent treatment and manipulation, security is diminished.

Unconditional Love – I don't believe parents intend to send the message to their children that their love is conditional. However, sometimes children get the impression—due to receiving more affirmation and affection when they're behaving in certain ways, such as getting good grades, doing their chores, or scoring goals—that the love they're receiving is based on their actions. That's conditional love and it's inherently insecure because the children don't know if they're always going to be able to live up to a standard that earns them the love they need. So, no matter what they do or don't do, say, or don't say, children must know they are loved no matter what. But how should they know they're loved? How should love be communicated?

Affirmation – Every child needs to hear the words "I love you," "I believe in you," and "I'm proud of you" from their parents.

Affection – When they are a baby or a toddler, a child needs cuddles and hugs and kisses. As they grow, they also need affectionate communication—tenderness and warmth rather than rudeness or harshness—in the way they are addressed by mom and dad.

Acceptance – A child may think, "Yes, my parents love me, but do they like me? They're not always giving me advice, putting me down, or making me feel less than just for being myself." What we often receive from friends—unconditional acceptance and a sense that it's OK to be ourselves—we also need from parents. Our parents need to take a curious stance with us and see who we become and how we see or experience the world.

Quality Time – Moms and dads who can't or don't want to spend time playing or teaching their children send a devaluing message. Children don't understand why mom or dad aren't around. They may just think they're not important enough to spend time with.

Discipline – If it's not done in anger, but rather in calmness, and if the message is sent that "it's your behaviour that's not acceptable, not you," then I think discipline sends a message to our children that, "mom and dad care how I turn out." That's a value message.

That's a pretty good list. Do you think it's true that every child needs such things? I would go a step further and say every child *deserves* such things. Not because they do anything, but because they're human, and every human needs and deserves these things.

Let's imagine we're born with this invisible air tank on our backs that's supposed to be filled up to 100% by mom and dad with all these ingredients of security. And let's say we had perfect parents who filled our tank to full. In that scenario we'd be well adjusted, wouldn't you say? We'd feel content, joyful and peaceful knowing that we're incredibly valuable and absolutely loveable. We'd likely be good communicators because we'd have no problems being open and vulnerable.

We wouldn't need anyone to like or love us, because we would already like and love ourselves. If others do too, that would be wonderful, but if not, that wouldn't change our experience of being loveable. We'd likely be good at conflict resolution because we'd have no problems admitting our faults and mistakes. Admitting such things wouldn't diminish our value.

We could give equal weight to other people's feelings, views and needs because again, that doesn't change our worth. There wouldn't be a lot of jealousy or strife in relationships because we could let everyone be who they are without needing them to conform to our standards to feel better about ourselves.

The problem, of course, is none of us have perfect parents so none of us get 100% of what we need from mom and dad. But it's air to the soul and we can't do without it, so we go looking for it from other sources. Perhaps we go looking to other people, such as grandparents, uncles, aunts, teachers, coaches, and youth leaders. Or maybe we look to siblings, friends, or girlfriends and boyfriends. In every interaction, in every relationship, we're looking for a sense that we are valuable and loveable for who we are. And, if we don't get these things anywhere, we must cope somehow.

To the degree we don't receive the elements of security anywhere is the degree that two things happen. First, we need to distract ourselves from the fact that our soul is suffocating. And the distractions of life are fun, but temporary in their satisfaction so they must be repeated over and over. That's what can lead to addictions. Things like smoking, drinking, drug use, sex, overeating, overworking, over-exercising, and a host of other coping strategies, are used to distract us from the fact that our souls just aren't receiving the value they need and deserve.

The second thing that happens when the soul doesn't get the air it needs and deserves is we have an enemy that latches onto us and flashes thoughts in our mind. Let's look at food for the soul.

SIGNIFICANCE – Soul Food

Significance is feeling important for what we do. We all need to know that we have something unique to offer the world. And our parents are supposed to help us find this too. Here's the ingredients that make up significance and how our parents can help us uncover it.

Purpose – Our parents are supposed to help uncover the path of *our* purpose for existing, not *their* purpose for us. If they push us down a path of their choosing, that's not in line with our passions and creativity, and we willingly go, it can lead to a lifetime of discontent or resentment. Unwillingness to go down a path chosen for us can lead to conflict and disconnection. We need to choose our own path.

Opportunities – Parents are to help us uncover our purpose by giving us opportunities to discover and develop our gifts and interests. That's partly why they sign us up for school, sports, music, dance, or whatever else we're interested in. They're helping us discover how our creativity should (or could?) be directed.

Praise – One of the things we need from the opportunities is for people to be proud of us, and we can see this need in children all the time. It comes through, "Hey dad, did you see that goal I scored?" or "Hey mom, look at this picture I drew for you," or "Did you see my report card?" Every child wants their parents to be proud of them, and there's nothing wrong with that. We're hardwired to need praise from our parents, and it affirms our significance in their eyes.

Mentoring – Another element we need in opportunities is coaching or training in how to improve our talents. The main message in the mentoring should be, "Hey, there's no such thing as failure, there's just an opportunity to learn" and "You fell off the bike, it's OK, get back up, you can do this" or "That's alright, you'll learn from this and be better next time."

Struggles – We need parents who will let us fail, fall, or lose. That's how we learn resiliency and strength, in picking ourselves back up. If moms and dads are overprotective and don't let us fall, they weaken our souls by robbing us of the chance to learn and grow. But they also need to teach us how to pick ourselves back up.

Choices – We all need age-appropriate choices because we have a will, and we want to use it. You see this early on in childhood. Children want to decide when they go to bed, what they wear, what they eat, etc. If parents are overcontrolling or have too many rules and harsh consequences, eventually children may become too dependent or rebellious.

My wife and I learned a lesson in this area when my oldest daughter, Alisha, was eleven years old. Every time my wife and I would ask or tell her to do something her go-to response was, "Why?" But she didn't want to know why; she wanted to say no, and "why" was a safer passive-aggressive way to say no. It drove her mother and I nuts, so we decided on an experiment. One day we said to her, "OK, Alisha, we're going to try something. Every day for the next month you will make every decision. We're not going to tell you to do anything, as long as three things happen: you have to get your schoolwork done; you have to eat healthy; and you have to get a good night's sleep. As long as those things get done, we won't interfere in your decisions." She was all over that.

The month was harder for us than her. But after two weeks she came to us and said, "Mom, Dad, I need you guys to tell me when to go to bed, because I just can't do it. I'm not getting enough sleep." So we asked her when she thought she should go to bed. She said ten o'clock and we said we'd make sure she was in bed by then. Every other decision she was fine with, and we stopped hearing the dreaded "why." We learned we needed to let off the clutch, because she was pushing the gas and getting frustrated.

Responsibilities – We need age-appropriate responsibilities because that helps us know mom and dad trust us. Having chores, jobs, or just being in charge of things helps children develop maturity and proficiency.

If we received all those things perfectly from mom and dad, we'd grow up to be pretty confident. We wouldn't be afraid to go off to school, start a company, or travel the world. We'd know we have something to offer the world and we'd want to use our talents to make a difference. We wouldn't be afraid to try new things because we'd either make an impact or learn a lesson.

But no one ever gets 100% of these things from mom and dad either. So, we go looking elsewhere. In high school we may try to achieve significance through sports, academics, or a unique appearance.

As adults we may become workaholics, and perhaps some of these people go home and can't get along with their partner, or can't get their child to listen to them. But these same adults go to work, they're affirmed, valued, promoted, and given raises. Everyone loves them at work. Why wouldn't they be workaholics? They're getting all the food for their soul from work and probably trying to get security from the money they make. It's the craziest thing—trying to get air from food. It's as silly as sticking a straw on a steak. You can't get air from food, but we humans try to get a sense of value for who we are from our jobs.

Too many times I find people who were over-affirmed for their significance and under-affirmed for their worth. This often led to a performance-based esteem. When transferred into a relationship this ethic can lead to a need to prove "I'm right and you're wrong" in this argument. That person can't admit to being wrong or their self worth takes a hit, and they can't afford that because they're already in the red.

SERVICE – Soul Water

It was Bob Dylan who sang "You gotta serve somebody," and he was right. We are built to serve, and we will serve someone or something. We will serve money, our families, our country, our community, ourselves, or our god, but we will serve because that's how we're designed. People usually serve who or what gives them the best sense of *Security* and *Significance*. If you're asking yourself who or what you serve, the answer may lie in how you spend your time or what you expend your energy on. We prioritize what we serve.

We are built like funnels for Love to flow into and out of. But if there's no outflow, then there's no room for more Love to come in. Service is the outflow of Love. It's how we demonstrate the difference that Love makes in our lives. In turn, that entices other funnels to serve and get Love flowing in and out as well.

Service is how we glorify Love, to highlight and magnify the beauty, splendour, and majesty of the character of Love. Service attracts people to the wonder that is Love. In a sense, service is the neon light sign directing people to Love's presence. Service then puts people in a heightened state of the awareness of Love. And a heightened awareness of the presence of Love changes people.

Love has a redemptive nature. By redemptive I mean Love brings us back from the dark into the light. Spirit brings us out of selfishness to selflessness. Spirit draws us from hiding to openness. Love challenges our conscience and cleans it, if we invite them to. And a clean conscience always wants to glorify the Spirit that cleaned it. The glorification of Love ignites the redemptive deposit they place in us and that in turn makes us want to partner with Love in redeeming others. That's why a redeemed funnel can't help but want to serve others, because that's the redemptive cycle Love has instituted. We are built to serve in our most authentic state.

There is meaningful service, aligned with our motivational gifts, or draining service. Service that makes a difference in the lives of others, that is congruent with our talents and passions, waters the soul. Service that is not in line with those things can burn us out. If we can make a living with the kind of service that waters, we will have a great life! If not, we at least need to find opportunities to serve in our personal lives for springs to flow in our hearts.

Ideally, as we're growing up, our parents will teach and model the place of service in our lives.

Our souls were designed by Love to need all these ingredients of soul-air security, soul-food significance, and soul-water service. And Spirit-parent wants to meet all our needs through our earthly parents.

The reason we're born with needs is because the purpose for all of us is the same. The biggest reason we're here is relationship—to know Love in an experiential way. Everything humans are good at or motivated to do—teach, lead, serve, give, nurture, administrate, build, etc.—would be almost entirely useless if there was only one person in the whole world. What we're gifted at and passionate about is only useful in the context of relationships. So, having needs propels us to relationships because Love knows it's only in the context of healthy relationships that we're ever going to get our needs met. And the first relationships Spirit puts us in to meet our needs are with mom and dad.

The needs we have were supposed to be filled by the people who brought us into the world and raised us. Some people received a lot of what they needed, while others did not. Some people's needs were left out and that creates a question mark on the soul. Others received the opposite of what they needed. They were abused, abandoned, and told through words and actions that they weren't that valuable or loveable and that creates a wound in the soul.

What does the soul do in this empty or wounded condition? It throws up a wall around itself to protect it from further hurt. The wall says to us, "I can protect you from hurt while giving you what you need." And everybody's wall is a bit different. It usually has to do with what we're good at.

I think Robin Williams was one of the funniest guys who ever lived. He also checked himself into rehab a few times with addiction issues. I believe Robin's wall was humour. His wall said, "I can get you the affirmation, attention, and affection your soul craves, and you won't have to let people in to see the real you. You'll be making them laugh, so they'll love you." But the wall lies to us all.

Not only does a wall not deliver what it promises—a pain-free life—but it actually makes things worse. If you think about it, walls invite more hurt than they stop. It's way easier to hurt someone you don't know than someone you do know. If someone cuts me off in traffic I may flip them the bird, honk, and scream. Why? Because I don't know them and it's easy to say or do hurtful things without a second thought. But if I looked over and that was my aunt...oops! I'd watch what I say or do then. If the ref makes a lousy call at the game, I may yell and scream at him. Why? Because I don't know him, and he doesn't know me, so there's no consequence to being an ass to him. However, if I look down and he looks back at me and I realize that's my next-door neighbour and I have to go home and face him...oops! Ya, I'd watch what I say then.

When we know someone, we guard what we say and do because we don't want to hurt them. Sure, if we hurt them, it can hurt more. But we can also use that as an opportunity to build a stronger relationship. If someone won't let you in to know the real them, you can't trust them or build a strong relationship. And in that scenario the walled-off person is not going to be able to experience the purpose of life—love-filled relationships. You can't have a close relationship with someone who won't let you see who they really are. You can't trust such a person.

Clearly the strategy of throwing up a wall for self-protection does not lead to a fulfilled life. Walls separate us from Love and are used by Love's enemies to destroy *supernatural mental health and relationships*. Walls contribute to miscommunication, hurt feelings, and division. The existence of a wall will require us to make up for the lack of *connection with Love*.

If we're not experiencing the true purpose of a rewarding life, then we'll have to cope somehow; and the coping strategies of life are often fun, but temporary in their satisfaction. They need to be repeated over and over to get the desired results. That's what makes them addictive. Drinking, drug use, overeating, sex, overworking, and a host of other habits are often used to distract the soul from the reality that it is suffocating, starving, and dehydrated.

Every child—every human being—needs and deserves all the ingredients of *Security, Significance,* and *Service*. Not because we do anything, but because we're humans. The soul knows what it needs and deserves, and it knows the difference between that and what it's getting.

If we believe that every human being is equally valuable, then it can't be what we look like, know, or do, or how people treat us that makes us valuable, because that's different for everyone. I think what makes anything valuable—like gold, diamonds, oil, or the Mona Lisa—is how little of it there is, who made it, and what it's useful for. Show me anything in this world there's little of that's useful for a lot of things and I'll show you something incredibly valuable. If there were only one iPhone in the world, everyone would want it.

There's only one of each of us. No one else is uniquely designed like you and no one else is living your story. We are useful for great accomplishments in leading, serving, giving, nurturing, building, teaching, and loving. And we were designed by the one who IS Love. That makes each of us incredibly valuable. And we love what we value.

When the soul doesn't get what it needs from healthy sources, it has enemies that latch on and flash thoughts in our minds. These enemies of Love are out to steal and destroy the creations of Spirit. If we're going to defeat such enemies, and *Reconnect with Love*, we must understand their tactics. So, let's take a closer look at our enemies to uncover how we can resist them in our minds.

Our Part:

Considering the needs-lists we just uncovered, look back at your own childhood. Now rate the people who raised or influenced you growing up on a scale of 1 to 10. How well did they do in giving you everything you needed and deserved? This isn't about blaming—as we've seen that's a cul-de-sac that leads us nowhere. This is about taking inventory. This is about uncovering unpaid debts that we'll look closer at later. This is also about coming to some "ah-ha" moments as to where we went looking for our needs. Perhaps the activities and involvements we thought were just about enjoyment or talents were also about coping with the fact that our soul was suffocating, starving, or dehydrated. The conclusions might lead us to realizations of what needs to be grieved or healed from our past.

SECTION TWO: The Enemies That Disconnect Us from Love

Chapter 4: The Enemy That Is Fear

First let me distinguish between thoughts and feelings. There is nothing inherently evil about any emotion we have. Fear, shame, and pride can be feelings we experience, and those emotions are useful messengers. Feelings alert us to the needs of the soul that are either being met or not. If we're feeling excited, happy, content or any other host of positive emotions, that's the soul telling us it's getting all that it needs in an interaction or situation right now. Figure out what those needs are and get more of them.

If we're feeling sad, lonely, angry, jealous, or any other host of emotions we don't like, that's the soul saying, "Hey, we have some needs we're not getting." Figure out what those needs are and either get them yourself or ask the people in your life to meet your needs. Feelings are to be listened to, so we get our needs met. Chasing them away with substance use or bad behaviour will just result in them coming back stronger. A cycle of bad habits or addictions can result.

The enemies we're going to expose now are not emotions. These enemies flash thoughts in our mind. Such thoughts can bring about emotions if we dwell on them, and that's what confuses us into taking responsibility for the thoughts when they're not really coming from our authentic selves. The thoughts are coming from the enemies of Love and it's important to distinguish that so we can take responsibility for resisting and replacing them.

We are not our enemies. We are not the problem. The problem is we don't know the real enemies, so we unwittingly become their pawns. As such, we allow them to flash unresisted thoughts in our mind and make deposits in our soul. Let's look at who the real enemies are, how they get in to attack us, and what they're up to in our minds. Then we can figure out how to resist and minimize their influence in our lives.

Enemy #1 – Fear

The number one enemy of Love is not Hate, as one might think. There is an old saying that goes, "Perfect Love casts out *Fear*." If Love is the kryptonite of Fear, then they are primary adversaries. When we don't receive all the ingredients of *Security* from healthy sources, the enemy latches onto our minds and flashes thoughts like, "Well, maybe you're not that valuable. Maybe you're not that important or loveable. Maybe you'll never get what you need from others. In fact, maybe people will hurt you, abuse you, abandon you or neglect and reject you. So, you better not trust people...you better not let them in." And so begins the disconnection from the sources Love wants to meet our needs through.

Ultimately our enemy wants to drive a wedge between us and the *Truth of* Love by having us develop unloving thought patterns. When we develop thought patterns that are contrary to Love—such as complaining, comparing, criticizing, or self-protective fantasizing—we unwittingly create hiding spots for *Fear*. Fear then has quick access to our thoughts when something goes wrong in our lives. From that perch in our mind *Fear* creates thoughts of doubt and distrust that drive us further away from Love. *Fear tells* us lies about Love and sews doubts in our minds as to whether we are loved or even loveable.

An important thing to note is that whatever this enemy is causing doubt about is already true! For example, years ago a man named Jesus was attacked by this enemy. The enemy said to him, "If you really are who you say you are, then do this for me." The truth was, he really was who he said he was. So, when the enemy that is *Fear* causes us to doubt our value and lovability...we can be certain the truth is, WE ARE VALUABLE AND LOVEABLE!

And, when we create walls to hide behind out of fear of being hurt, we take the place of Love in our lives because Spirit wants to be the fortress we run to for protection from the *enemies*. Trying to do Love's job in our hearts and minds gives the keys of the castle to the enemy. Once the enemy has the keys and resides behind the strongholds in our minds, it's not too difficult to cloud our view of the truth of who we are and why we exist.

Fear's thoughts ignite our feelings of fear, and no one likes those feelings, so we try to get rid of them. And the ways we try to get rid of them never work.

Here's a tactic of the enemy we need to be aware of and vigilant against: Our enemy gives us a real problem and then hands us a fake solution to fix the problem, so we never get rid of the enemy or the problem. The real problem is becoming disconnected with Love—our designer and most trustworthy friend. Let's look at some of the false solutions Fear gives us to fix that problem that never work.

People Pleasing. How we're treated growing up often propels us down one of two paths. The first path can be viewed as "loving in order to love." That path starts with a high sense of security from being loved well. That person is filled up with love and just wants to give life from a full heart. They don't need anything in return. If someone loves them back, great. If not, they keep giving to those who show value for the gift of love.

The other path can be defined as, "loving in order to be loved." That path begins with some emptiness. The person is missing some key elements of security, so they serve, give, compliment, etc. to get something back. If they don't get back what is sought after or desired, they may serve more in hopes of eventual extraction. They may also get discouraged or burned out from constantly giving, and abandon "loving" altogether.

The challenge for everyone joining in a relationship with people on these two paths is they both look the same from the outside. They're both perceived as giving, generous, and loving with their time, words, and actions. However, one is loving and the other one is engaged in manipulation, which isn't really love.

Remember, the real problem is not knowing through faith, intellect, and experience, the true nature of Love and how valuable and loveable we are. So, the enemy's fake solution is to pursue the esteem of others to fix that problem. The subconscious thinking becomes, "If I can just get everyone else to like me, I'll feel better about myself. That way I'll have less fear and more security."

Hence, some people spend their lives as passive communicators, giving everyone what they want and valuing other people's needs over their own. They roll over, serve, and give to a fault in hopes of ensuring no one is mad at them and everyone approves of them. But in the end this tactic doesn't work because they're just stuffing down their own needs and they soon realize no one else ever serves, gives, and "loves" them the way they do for others. That leads them back to the conclusion they're not that valuable or loveable. The results are often emotional exhaustion, discouragement, anxiety, and depression. The enemy—Fear—still wins, in that we're still not connected to Love and still don't walk in our true nature of value and lovability.

Anger. When Fear shows up, Anger (the enemy that leads to our emotion) comes along and says, "I can help you get rid of Fear. Just get mean, intimidating, loud, aggressive, passive aggressive or even violent. Then you'll put people in their place, and they'll respect you, adhere to you, follow you, and you'll never feel fear again." The problem with going along with Anger is that it's not really trying to get rid of fear. They're buddies attempting to do the same thing—destroy our chances of loving relationships and getting our needs met. You can't have a close trusting relationship with an angry person. Anger alienates everyone around, leaving the person alone and left with, "I'm clearly not that valuable or loveable." And we're right back to Fear winning again.

Controlling. Control is deceptively attractive because it's a bit of a double-edged sword. On the one hand, self-control is a good thing that leads to self-respect. However, in attempting to get rid of Fear we seek to control other people's opinions or behaviour and circumstances we have no ability to control and have no business trying to. Sometimes we use the other solutions of people pleasing or anger to control people's impressions and treatment of us. We've seen why that doesn't work. Other times we try to control through rules and regulations, policies and procedures, or judgement and criticism. In the end these tactics don't work either because they either show us to be hypocrites who can't adhere to our own demands of others, or they just frustrate and alienate everyone around us. Life inevitably gives us circumstances and people we cannot control and that leads to frustration and resignation. Again, we're left with Fear's desired conclusion of our lack of worth and lovability.

Fads and Trends. The best place to hide a yellow pencil is not amongst a bunch of black pens. The best place to hide that pencil is amongst a bunch of other yellow pencils that look just like it. Our enemy knows this, so Fear conceals Truth amongst a bunch of other solutions that have the appearance of wisdom but lack true power to fix our real problem. It wouldn't be in line with Love's heart for me to point out specifics here and shame anyone by attacking sacred cows. However, a word of caution...always be leery of joining in popular trends. The enemy likes to repackage old trends for each generation.

Many people—especially men—do not want to acknowledge the presence of Fear in their lives. Either we see that as weak or it's because we don't experience the emotion of fear. It's important to recognize that the influence of the enemy Fear does not necessitate the presence of the emotion of fear. But if worry or anxiety are factors in your life, then the enemy that is Fear may be a factor. Other signs Fear is influencing us, or running the show, are the existence of addictive thinking and behaviour, relational strife, jealousy, lust, envy, overeating, hatred, grudges, and bitterness.

Fear brings worry, anxiety and depression and robs us of the joy of Love. Fear makes us weak and tired. Fear cannot fulfill our needs or restore our peace. There is no contentment in Fear. It only has lies, doubt and disconnection from all that is good for us and about us. It also brings with it another two-headed monster to wreak havoc in our lives. That enemy is called *Pride*.

Our Part:

Ask Love to open the eyes of your heart and reveal previous blind spots. Look back and take stock of how *Fear* has affected you over the years. When did it first come along for you while growing up? What did it lead you to do in life and relationships? What are the thought patterns you've allowed to develop that give *Fear* a stronghold hiding spot from which to launch attacks?

In my own life, I have been blindsided and hurt so many times I developed a thought pattern to let *Fear* hide. Many times, when I have a *Fear* thought I will then have a future conversation with someone and play out in my mind all that person might say so I'll have a suitable answer. *Fear* tells me if I just think it out ahead, I won't get blindsided and hurt. But those future conversations rarely happen, and if they do, they never pan out the way I've pre-played them in my head. I've rarely prevented myself from being blindsided and hurt fantasizing about future conversations. All I've really accomplished is wasted current moments that I could have been enjoying. In those moments *Fear* pushes me away from entrusting my future to Love. Love is wise, all-knowing, and has never been blindsided. Spirit wants to use all that happens to me to teach, build, bless, and advance my character. And Spirit knows sometimes that will involve discomfort or pain.

What has *Fear* been telling you in your relationships, friendships, workplace, and home life? What does it whisper to you when conflicts arise? What does it say about you when you make mistakes or hurt someone? And what tactics have you tried at various stages in your life to try and minimize or delete the feeling of insecurity that *Fear* has contributed to? The answers may lead you to discover what needs to heal in your life to kick *Fear* to the curb.

Chapter 5: The Enemy That Is Pride

Enemy #2 – Pride

Pride doesn't care what you think about yourself so long as you think of yourself in comparison to others, or some standard others tell you to live up to. Comparison is the weapon of Pride. We all have comparative thoughts and use comparative language. If someone uses terms like "good" or "great," "ugly" or "beautiful," "smart" or "dumb" to describe themselves, I could ask "Compared to who or what?" We mock, belittle, condescend, and judge all in the will of Pride's comparisons.

There are two equally deceitful cohorts within the enemy that is Pride. If we compare ourselves to others, or a standard, and we're better, we're falling prey to the deceiver called *Arrogance*. If we compare ourselves to others, or a standard, and we're worse, we're victims of the deceiver called *Shame*.

Arrogance

I always get a kick out of someone calling me, or anyone else, arrogant. When we call someone arrogant—or any other degrading name—we're implying, "you're that, and I'm not" (If we thought we were that too, we wouldn't feel the need to point it out to someone else). That says, "I'm better than you" (at least in the moment). Ironically, that is the very definition of arrogance!

Arrogance pushes people away with messages like, "You don't need anyone to tell you what to do," "You've got this covered," and "You can figure this out on your own." *Arrogance gives us a false sense of confidence, and a real sense of insecurity.* It suggests to us that we're somehow less than competent, capable, wise, or enough if we take advice, ask for help, or admit faults and failures. We can't have healthy relationships while walking with *Arrogance*, because we won't let people in or communicate that we need them.

Arrogance empowers blind spots, and we all have blind spots. The problem with allowing *Arrogance* to hide our unloving character traits or habits is it then usually takes a very negative and hurtful event to reveal them. In essence, we usually have to be humiliated in some way to see what needs to change about us.

As a young man, I was put in charge of youth programs for a non-profit community organization. In my youthful exuberance, I introduced new programs and ways of doing things, and the youth loved them. But my success went to my head. I remember sitting in a board meeting of older men who had been running this organization for years. In my excited report of all that was going on due to my leadership, I began to criticize them for what I believed to be their complacency or apathy. Understandably, that didn't go over well with them. One well-respected man in the community, who was on that board, began to address my criticism. I don't remember everything he said. I just remember excusing myself after he was finished, going into the bathroom, and bawling my eyes out in humiliation. I'd like to say that was the last time I was ever humiliated due to the influence of *Arrogance* in my life, but nothing could be further from the truth. I have had to learn the hard way a lot in my life. What I've learned is, we have a choice in life—we can either *humble ourselves* or *be humiliated*. Both are tough. But *Humiliation* is worse! *Arrogance* is a real relationship killer.

Arrogance descends on us like dew every morning. We don't have to look for it. No one ever says, "I've been searching for more *Arrogance*, but I just can't find it anywhere." No one needs to work at being more arrogant. It comes naturally to all of us. If you don't think that statement is true for you, guess what's blocking your view of the truth? Often, an organization or movement begins in great humility, such as the twelve-step programs or some spiritual awakening movements. But it's not long before *Arrogance* attacks participants and the initial power of humility is neutralized. Control, in-fighting, and disunity often results when *Arrogance* infiltrates.

Arrogance wants us to focus on Respect and Reputation. Don't get me wrong, there's nothing wrong with gaining respect and having a great reputation. Both are admirable to have earned. But that's the point: both need to be earned for them to be admirable. In effect, neither of them is any of our business while we're living our lives in front of others. When *Arrogance* gets us to pursue them, rather than pursue Love-infused character and integrity, we champion all the wrong things. We become self-promoters, braggarts, boasters, and blowhards. We worry that people really don't know what we have to offer. We fret that we won't get opportunities to show what we can do, so we won't receive longed-for promotions or advancements. *Arrogance* only strengthens *Fear*. The irony is, the ones being affected by *Arrogance* often look like, and believe, *confidence* has driven away *Fear*. Nothing could be further from the truth.

Arrogance blocks Unity. As we'll see later, the power of Love, in part, comes from the *mutual submission* that leads to absolute unity. *Arrogance* works hard to disrupt such unity. *Arrogance* inspires its victims to promote the *differences* of their intellect or abilities, rather than *commonalities* of their heart with others. If one person perceives another as better than them in some way, in the absence of earned respect and admiration, the first person isn't likely to feel safe to entrust themselves and connect with the arrogant person. So, *unity*, and the *power of Love*, is negated by *Arrogance*.

Shame

The enemy that is *Shame* is different than the emotions of shame. Shame feels like embarrassment or humiliation. The enemy *Shame* flashes thoughts in our minds. It's also necessary to distinguish *Shame* from *Guilt*.

Guilt says, "*What* you did was wrong. Don't do that again." That message comes through our conscience and it's useful to help us change into better people. But *Shame* says, "*Who* you are is wrong. You're not enough." That's a destructive message because we can't change who we are, and it's a lie anyway.

Shame tells us we're not as *blank* as we need to be, or as other people are. "You're not as pretty, you're not as funny, you're not as smart, you're not as successful, you're not as popular, you're not as competent, you're not as valuable or lovable as *blank*." It also says, "If anyone knew how less than you really are, if they knew what you were really thinking, feeling, doing or all about, then they would judge you, condemn you, abandon you, reject you and never give you the respect, affection, attention and love you need. So, you better hide who you really are and what you're really thinking and doing. You better not let anyone see the real you."

No one likes to feel the emotions that go with *Shame's* thoughts, so we try to get rid of them. Sometimes we go the opposite direction to walk with *Arrogance* for a while. We may puff ourselves up by showing off or bragging. Or perhaps we live life in an "I'll show you" fiercely independent way. "I'll show you I'm enough, strong, smart, funny, successful, or competent." That kind of striving leads to exhaustion as we try to fill the holes in our soul by digging another hole. Or maybe we just turn the attention to others.

The language of *Shame* is *blame*. Another way we try to get rid of *Shame* is by focusing on the faults, failures, shortcoming, or transgressions of others. Any time I witness a person name-calling, criticizing, blame-shifting or bullying another human being I know the person doing it is being affected by *Shame*. Sometimes the only way we can think of to stop feeling less than is to put someone else down with our minds, mouth, or attitude.

In the long run, such tactics never help us feel better about ourselves. At some level we know our actions go against our true nature and our conscience bothers us. Even if we've seared our conscience through habitual hypocrisy, *Shame* leaves a mark.

Every time we are shamed by others, or are agents of *Shame* for others, *Shame* leaves a deposit in us. Whether what we were shamed for was true or a lie, whether the accusation was audible or implied, unless we actively resisted at that moment, *Shame* deposits a virus in our soul. That way *Shame* has a means to attack our minds in the future. This is why learning to *speak the Truth in Love*, and to forgive ourselves, is so important.

So, the enemies of Love, and our souls, are exposed as *Fear, Shame, and Arrogance*. These enemies are out to destroy relationships because they know it's only in the context of healthy relationships that we're ever going to get our needs met. Those needs—*Security, Significance, and* Service—are the resources Love has to offer us through other people. Receiving those needs through Love's designed sources is the only way to walk in the Truth of how valuable and loveable we are, as well as fulfill Love's purpose for our lives.

The enemies block the path to our desired destination through lies and doubts and then tempt us to follow a dead-end road. They deceive us into believing we are the source of love, we can earn love through fearful tactics such as *people pleasing, control, manipulation, and enlightenment*. Then all our striving leads to disappointment, failures, and an even wider chasm between us and the one who IS Love, not to mention the truth of who we are and why we're here. That's why it's so important that we *Reconnect with Love* and learn to resist our enemies using the tools that Love gives us.

Much more could be said about the nature and ploys of our enemies. For example, Brené Brown writes extensively and admirably about *Shame* and its effects on our lives in all her books. However, for our purposes, we've given enough attention to the enemies. Let's find effective ways to deal with them so *Supernatural Mental Health* and *Relationships* can grow. For that to happen, we must start with the true path to *Reconnect with Love*.

Our Part:

Ask Love to show you how *Arrogance* and *Shame* have affected your mental health, addictions, and your attitudes and behaviour in relationships. Think about how you've tried to get rid of this enemy's influence without much success. Think of past hurt and unhealed wounds as the portals through which your enemies attack.

SECTION THREE: How to Reconnect with Love

Chapter 6: Reconnect through Healing

If you think you can hold on to grudges, resentment, unforgiveness, bitterness, or unresolved losses, and still move forward and have great mental health and relationships, you are kidding yourself. It'll never happen. Our souls are not built that way. Such things not only serve as footholds for our enemies, but they also block the passage for Love to flow through us. Wounds must be healed, and losses must be grieved, in order for Love to build *supernatural mental health* in us and vitalize our *relationships*.

I call it *healing,* and not *forgiveness*, for a reason. If someone asks for your forgiveness because they're sorry and want to make things right with you, then you are giving forgiveness. That seems fair, or just, because they are showing remorse and demonstrating they want to change. But if someone isn't asking for your forgiveness and not showing remorse, to be told you need to forgive them doesn't seem fair, or just. We have a negative inner reaction to that because it seems like we're being asked to endorse their treatment of us and let them get away with it.

But just because the person isn't asking for forgiveness or changing doesn't mean you're doomed to hang on to resentments that can easily turn to bitterness and rob you of joy. You can still heal and move on. I call it *Grace Healing*. Grace means giving someone good when they deserve bad. When we give Grace to heal, we're doing it because it's the best thing to do for *us* so that Love can resume flowing in and out of us.

Four Steps of Grace Healing

There are four steps of *Grace Healing* revealed in a parable Jesus taught. Allow me to paraphrase it for you. (There will be a test later, so please pay attention to the details.)

Back in the day, when there were masters and servants, a certain master was owed today's equivalent of a million dollars. This was in the days when his servant was making a dollar per day in wages. One day the master said to his court staff, "Hey, this guy owes me a lot of money. I'm tired of waiting to be paid. Let's get him in here to settle the account."

When the servant was brought in, his master said, "You've racked up quite a debt. It's time to pay me for everything you owe me. If you can't pay me today, I'm going to throw you in jail, sell all your stuff, and then sell you and your family into slavery to settle the debt." His servant was mortified and fell to his knees. He wept and pleaded his case to his master. "Please, my lord," he cried. "Please be patient with me. I'll pay you everything I owe you, just give me more time." After a lot more sobbing, pleading and explaining by the servant, the master developed compassion for his servant and said, "OK, I have decided to wipe out your entire debt. You no longer owe me anything. You are free to go."

Now that same servant was himself a master to his own servant. And he remembered that his servant owed him today's equivalent of ten dollars. His servant was making fifty cents per day. So, he said to his guards, "Hey, this servant of mine owes me ten dollars. Let's get him in here to settle his account." When the servant was brought in the master said to him, "It's time to pay me everything you owe me, or I'll put you in jail, sell your stuff, and sell you and your family into slavery to pay your debts." His servant fell to his knees and pleaded, "Please, my lord, be patient with me. I'll pay you everything I owe you, just give me more time." However, that servant/master refused to listen and sent his servant off to jail. Proceedings were started to sell his possessions to pay his debt.

When the original master heard what his servant had done, he called the man back to his court. He said, "You wicked servant. I forgave you all your debt and you couldn't forgive a small debt of your own servant? I have changed my mind. You will now be taken off to prison and I'll sell your stuff to cover your debts."

Here's the test. Why couldn't a servant, who has just been forgiven a million-dollar debt, forgive his own servant for a ten-dollar debt? You'd think he'd have left his master's court in jubilation and been the most generous soul in town: a veritable Ebenezer Scrooge reborn. But instead, he was stubborn and miserly, judgmental, and unmoved by the plight of others. Why? The answer is in the details.

Did you notice what each servant asked for of their masters? They asked for more time to pay off their debts. Is it possible, when you're making a dollar per day, to pay off a million dollars in debt? Not if you worked your whole life, right? So that servant was asking out of *arrogance*, not *humility*. He was operating in self-righteousness, believing he could pay off that debt. Perhaps he then engaged in critical judgement of his servant to show that he deserved to have his debts forgiven by his master. Maybe he thought he'd show the world how diligent a manager he was by being strict. After all, there are policies and procedures to follow. We have rules and regulations for a reason.

Here's an important principle to remember when it comes to healing the past: We can't give what we don't have or haven't acquired somewhere. If we haven't received forgiveness, it's going to be more difficult to give it to others when necessary. If another person hasn't worked through their healing issues, they are probably still affected by the enemies—*Fear, Shame, and Arrogance*. That means they are more likely to be agents of those enemies, who promote enemy messages. If we don't heal our issues, then we are more likely to be agents of the enemies in other people's lives. When we heal our issues, our hearts are softened towards those who have hurt us. Making things right with others releases the flow of Love to that individual, as well as others.

Also, did you notice the four steps of *Grace Healing* found in this parable? Let's take a closer look.

Step One: Acknowledge There Is a Debt

The first master said to those around him, "This guy owes me a lot of money." That's an important acknowledgement when it comes to healing. As we've seen from the ingredients of *Security* and *Significance*, we need and deserve a lot of things to walk in the truth of how valuable and loveable we are. The soul knows what it needs and deserves, and it knows the difference between that and what it's getting. The difference represents a debt. The soul indebted to, that's not being paid, gets anxious and depressed. It's like a sponge that's been stepped on for years—it has no air in it and doesn't bounce back easily.

It's usually obvious to most people that they didn't receive all they needed and deserved from family or friends. However, some either minimize the past through rose-coloured glasses, thinking they've moved on, or reason it's pointless to revisit because it can't be changed. They may even think they're being compassionate by not saying anything to those who left elements out of their early years. They say to themselves that since they never think of the past it clearly doesn't affect them. That's kind of like saying the electricity in this room doesn't affect me because I can't see the wires and don't notice the power. Well, just turn off the light switch and see if the power is affecting you. Just because we don't think of something often doesn't mean it doesn't affect us.

Others conclude their parents did the best they could and so there's no debt. Or maybe they know they got more love and support than other children, so they just let what they didn't get go, without making a fuss. That's like me telling you we're going diving and I want to show you this sunken ship at the bottom of the inlet. To get down there, look around, and then return to the surface, I tell you that you're going to need a full tank of air. So, I instruct you to go across the street and inquire which vendor can fill your tank to one hundred percent full. You go over to the first vendor, and she says she only has enough air to put sixty-five percent in your tank. Then you go to the second guy, and he says he can give you eighty percent. When you complain to him, he says, "What are you talking about? It's the best you're going to get and it's better than sixty-five percent." It might be the best they can do, but in proportion to what you need, you're still going to die on our trip without one hundred percent.

Just because our parents did the best they could doesn't mean we received all that we needed. And, if we didn't get all that we needed and deserved as valuable human beings, then our soul is owed a debt. When there's an outstanding debt to the soul, not only is it weakened, but it becomes vulnerable to attacks by our enemies. The debt must be acknowledged to be healed.

Step Two: Give Your Soul Compassion and a Voice by Confronting the Debtors

Why did the original master need to haul his servant into court if he was just going to forgive the debt anyway? Wouldn't it have been more timesaving to just say, "This guy owes me a lot of money, but I'm just going to let it go?" Perhaps that would have saved time, but it wouldn't have been honest or honouring to himself.

Let's say I walk up to you right now and slap you across the face and run away. And let's assume you don't run after me to choke me out. Then I see you next week and you're scowling at me. So, I come over to you and say, "Ah, are you still upset about that slap? Get over it. Let's go play tennis." If you come play tennis with me and you never say anything to me about the fact that I disrespected, dishonoured, and hurt you, then your silence is kind of agreeing that you didn't deserve to be treated any better. You might think you're being the bigger person. You might think you don't want to rock the boat, or further damage our friendship, so you just stay quiet. But you're not being the bigger person. You are subtly playing into the hands of your enemy, *Shame*.

Remember, *Shame* wants you to feel less than. The people in your past who didn't give you all that you needed and deserved made you feel less than. If you don't stand up for your value and equal worth to those people, your silence is agreement. Your silence proclaims, "I didn't deserve the needs I didn't get." Your silence gives a foothold to *Shame*. Every time you are accused of being less than, by people's actions, words, or lack thereof, *Shame* leaves a deposit—a little virus in your soul so it can resend old messages into new relationships. To weaken Shame's ability to use the past to attack you, you have to say something—you must speak the truth of Love. But the *How* of the confrontation is crucial.

Often when someone goes directly to the person that hurt them, they do so to extract an apology, gain some empathy or compassion, and change the nature of the relationship. That can be seen as manipulation rather than loving. If you need a specific response from the person you're confronting, and not getting it will make you feel worse, then it's not likely you're giving your soul the compassion it needs. Besides, too many times a direct confrontation is received poorly. An altercation done the wrong way, for the wrong reasons, usually won't lead to the kind of healing we need.

You don't even need the other person's involvement in the type of confrontation I'm speaking of. Remember, the point is to give your soul a voice and compassion, not change the other person. That's why most of the time I recommend writing letters. Letters you're never going to send, so it's safe to say anything you need to. The letters can be read to a counsellor, trusted friend, or to the one who IS Love. The purpose is to speak the truth of Love about your feelings, needs and worth. The result is usually cathartic. Then, having given yourself a compassionate voice, it's time to move to the next step of the *Grace Healing* process.

Step Three: Develop Compassion for the Debtor

In the parable, when faced with a sobbing, pleading servant—regardless of his arrogant motives—the original master felt compassion. Admittedly, when we confront our debtors through letters, they are not pleading for our forgiveness. Nevertheless, the third step is still crucial. We must see each person through the eyes of compassion.

In the dynamics of unforgiveness we are usually above the other person. We say to ourselves, "I could never act like that" or "I would never treat someone like that." In other words, we're engaged in *Pride's* tactic of comparison, and we are thinking of ourselves as better than that person. But that's a lie. We're not better than the people who hurt us. We're not worse either. We're just different.

We're different because we weren't raised by their parents. We didn't have their influences and experiences. And we aren't affected by the enemies, *Fear* and *Pride*, in the same ways they are. But for *Grace Healing* to take place we must admit that if all those factors were the same for us, we could have hurt someone just like they did. That's part of summoning the incredible power of Humility that we'll expand on in a subsequent chapter.

The chances are almost certain that your debtors were attacked by *Fear* and *Pride* at some point in their life, to become the kind of person that could hurt you. When the people that hurt you were five years old, playing in the playground with their friends, I guarantee you they never said to them, "When I grow up, I want to take a child and completely devastate or leave them feeling worthless." They didn't come out of the womb the way you experienced them. Something happened to them along the way to turn them into the kind of person that could wound you. Figuring out how they have been attacked by *Fear* or *Shame* through investigation or extrapolation is necessary to develop the kind of compassion that can lead to *Grace Healing*.

Your debtors are like empty wells. They probably didn't receive all they needed either. And you can't give what you didn't receive or gain along the way. You can go to an empty well every day hoping for water. You can get angry at it, kick it, swear at it, and resent it. But it's never going to have water for you.

Through genuinely curious wondering or investigating how your debtors got to be who they are, you develop softness towards them. By stepping into their shoes and thinking how *Fear, Shame, and Arrogance* have and are affecting them, you develop compassion. The truth is likely that your debtors were victims themselves, long before they were victimizing or leaving you empty. They are to be pitied rather than resented. When your soul gets there, you're ready for the fourth step of *Grace Healing*.

Step Four: Consciously and Continually Decide to Let the Debt Go

This is a step where we can't "fake it 'til we make it." We can't fool or trick our soul into being ready. We'll know when we get there. But the decision to let a debt go sometimes isn't a "one-off." Sometimes letting go is a gradual process and sometimes we must stand up to our enemies badgering us about the past after our initial decision.

Love lets us go through what we call tests to show us where we're at in the healing process. Such tests must not be seen as "pass/fail" scenarios. The tests are best thought of as GPS coordinates to show us where we are versus where we need to go.

Fear, Shame, and Arrogance will use current circumstances to trigger old wounds and feelings. If we succumb to the temptation to pick up past hurts and undesired feelings, we may think we're right back where we started and get discouraged. In that case we need to reframe the discouragement as a sign that we care and have grown. There was likely a time when we wouldn't have been bothered by those thoughts and feelings. The fact that going back discourages us is an ironic sign that we have moved forward in some way. Reflect on the lessons to be learned and then stand up to those enemies with a truth claim like, "I have healed from that, and I will not pick up resentment and hurt again. The truth is, I have compassion for myself and that person. The truth is a person's hurtfulness was about them and their enemies, not me. As for me, I have let go of that debt."

If the Spirit of Love is present during this process, then at the end we feel a lightness of soul and a renewed hope to move forward in peace. We have effectively constructed a shield around our minds and hearts against the attacks of our enemies. Our hearts are softened towards the people that have hurt us. But this isn't the end of *Grace Healing*. There is another phase that must take place for Love to flow through us freely.

Making Things Right

It is often the case that when we have been hurt, we have hurt people back. That may have been through our words, actions, or silence. It may also have been through our attitudes. We sometimes cut people out of our lives emotionally, relationally, and physically. We may tell ourselves it's because of a healthy boundary and self-love. But really, it's about self-protective *Fear*.

Fear sends our minds all kinds of deceptive thoughts to hinder the flow of Love through us and prevent us from knowing and experiencing our true identity and purpose. Those ideas might include, "How you treated them was a natural reaction to being hurt. They started it and they're just reaping what they sowed. You did nothing wrong in what you said or did. Anyways, it's over now that you've forgiven them." Even though our healing journey has so far led to softness of heart to the offender, *Fear* knows we're still blocked up to the flow of Love until we make amends.

For many years my mom said things that wounded me deeply. Over the years I discovered such wounds were at the heart of some addictive thinking and behaviour. I became aware of *Shame's* messages to my mind and started to alter how I reacted to them. Then I went through the four steps of *Grace Healing* and softened towards my mom. But I kept her at arm's length. I could be around her and not incur further offense and resist the urge to take up past offenses. But I still wouldn't let her into my heart and that hindered me from feeling love for her.

Recently, Spirit showed me my part in the problem and convinced me to humble myself and make things right with her. After saying my peace to her and getting kind forgiveness, Love has been flowing through me to her in renewed ways. I then made things right with several other people from my past that I'd forgiven but kept at arm's length too. The newness of Love flowing in and out of me is incredibly refreshing each day. And I now hear, see, and feel Spirit in ways I never had before.

In my counselling sessions, I'm giving the wisdom and guidance of Spirit that is beyond my understanding and capabilities. It's as if I'm co-creating with Love to make new paths for people in their thinking and behaving. *Making things right* unclogs us to complete the process of *Grace Healing* and enables us to be a partner in Spirit's great plan.

Our Part:

Think of all the people in your life that you needed and deserved elements of *Security* and *Significance* from who didn't give them to you. These could be parents, stepparents, siblings, disloyal friends, ex-partners, bullies, or abusers. It may have been from commission—hurting you with their words or actions—or through omission—not giving you what you needed due to absence or ignorance. If you have not yet dealt with these hurts or losses in an assertive way using the four steps of *Grace Healing*, there's work to be done.

Write each person a two-part letter that you're never going to send. In the first part, pour out your thoughts and feelings about what they did or didn't do that wounded you. Let them have it, and share how it impacted you then and for your journey since.

Warning: This is going to drum up some undesired feelings. You may become sad, angry, anxious, or even depressed. Such feelings are natural and useful. Remember, most things that grow in this world need fertilizer. That's crap. Our souls are no different. We need to go *through* crap to grow and become stronger. If we walk around or away from the tough circumstances of life and never deal with them, we're pushing the pause button on the growth of our soul. The soul not growing becomes anxious, depressed, and weak. However, if such feelings lead to thoughts of self-harm, then pause the exercise. Recognize these thoughts are from your enemies. They do not want to let go. They do not want you to enjoy the freedom of healing. Stand up to them by speaking some truth about the good that you are capable of and then resume the exercise.

Once you have completed the first part of the letter then think about the idea that this person reads your letter and responds perfectly. If this person were to receive your letter with humility and contrition, and respond to you, what would be so great for you to hear them say? Write that down—a perfect response to you from them. That shows what's in your heart and what you need. Then read your letters and responses to either a trusted friend or counsellor to receive the empathy and compassion you need and deserve. Process your thoughts and feelings before you move on to step three of *Grace Healing*.

Next, to develop compassion for your offenders, do some investigating where possible. Put together questions to ask relatives or friends of your debtors and figure out how they got to be this person. If interviews are not possible or safe, then simply wonder to yourself how *Fear* and *Shame* have affected them and what those enemies have been telling them over the years. Perhaps your actions or reactions were triggers for the enemies' messages to that offender. Write these thoughts out too.

Don't succumb to blame, as that's just the language of *Shame*. You didn't do anything to deserve hurt. Remember, you are incredibly valuable and loveable because you are a creation of the one who IS Love and you are designed to have Love flow in and out of you to others. Your worth stems from the uniqueness of your design and story! This exercise is about true understanding that can lead to sympathy or empathy for those who hurt you. That is essential for the healing process to take root in your soul.

When I go to the gym to become stronger, I don't go to easy weights. I go to difficult weights to show and develop strength. The same can be said of the soul. If we want to develop and display strength of character, we need to do the difficult things. Which is easier, to have compassion for victims or to develop compassion for victimizers? If we want to grow and show strong souls, we must acknowledge the equal value of those who hurt us and get inside their minds and hearts to figure out what they needed that they weren't getting that led them to follow *Fear, Shame, and Arrogance* and hurt us.

Now it's time to choose to let the debt go. Have a little ceremony where you burn your letters as a physical symbol of your inner decision to release the offense.

Our Part:

When it comes to making amends, think of anyone you have cut off, shut down to, criticized or judged, or treated with less love than you ought to have. Now write them a letter taking responsibility for your part in the divide. Tell them what they deserved to get from you but didn't. Tell them what they got from you that they didn't deserve. Tell them how sorry you are. If it's safe, you are able, and it would do no harm, send them the letter, and ask for their forgiveness. If you can't or won't send it, then at least read it to someone who cares about you as a role play. Get it off your heart somehow.

Chapter 7: Reconnect through Humility

Years ago, I gave a speech on Humility. Not long after that I was humiliated on several occasions. I drew a direct correlation and resolved never to speak on the subject again. It was as if Spirit said, "Oh yeah, you think you have a handle on humility, do you?" and then proceeded to teach me a lesson. And yet, here I am writing about it again.

I'm willing to risk it because I believe humility is the gateway to wisdom and great relationships. If two people are acting in complete humility towards one another, it would be impossible for them not to get along. Humility allows Love to flow through, transform, unite, and empower all those who utilize it. And humility is misunderstood and underutilized these days.

Humility is one of those ironic traits that as soon as you claim to have obtained it, you've just lost it. I think that dynamic and our aversion to being humiliated has kept us away from a thorough study and understanding of the subject.

So, I've come to view humility as a coat we need to put on every day—much like the invisibility cloak of Harry Potter fame—rather than a trait we can claim to have acquired permanently. Unlike arrogance, that seems to fall on us each morning like dew, humility requires a more purposeful approach.

Humility can be defined as a marriage between two other "H" words—honesty and honour. By *honesty* I mean an acknowledgement of all that we're capable of, both good and bad. And by *honour,* I mean treating something with the value it deserves. We'll look at those characteristics more as we go, and we'll look at some ways to put on humility later. For now, let's focus on how this powerful tool can be useful in our efforts to *Reconnect with Love*.

Use Humility to Experience the Transformation of Love

Love changes a person. They make us want to be the best versions of ourselves. We don't need to be the best versions of ourselves to earn Love's presence. They take care of the cleaning. We just need to come to Love on their terms. The terms and transformation of Love comes through *surrender*, and that can't happen without *humility*.

We put on *humility* by acknowledging our actions, thoughts, words, and attitudes often fall short of the nature of Love. We put on *humility* by admitting that the lack of Love in our lives has led to disastrous consequences for us and those we relate to. And we realize we have all been victimized by others who operate outside of Spirit's nature.

If Love had been in charge of our lives—leading, guiding, protecting, providing, correcting, and teaching us—then our lives would have been filled with a whole lot more joy and peace. That doesn't mean that having Spirit in charge of our lives will lead to a trouble-free life. But with Spirit in charge, trials can lead to great growth and increased love.

There is no *Fear* in Love. There is no risk or danger when Love is in charge. Putting Spirit in charge of our lives doesn't mean we have no responsibility or work to do. It just means we have an anchor in times of trouble. It means we have a best friend to talk to all the time who knows everything and cares deeply about us. It means we have the incredible resources at our disposal to create and succeed at whatever Love leads us to accomplish.

Putting Love in charge of our lives also doesn't mean we have to clean up our act or have it all together. The *humility* of Spirit never compares us to anyone else except the nature of Love. Spirit never uses *Fear* or *Shame* to motivate us to change. We never have to impress Love by trying to be someone or something we're not. Instead, Spirit uses acceptance, kindness, and grace to transform our conscience and behaviour. In short, there's literally no downside to inviting Love to be in charge of our lives. There's only blessings or lessons with Spirit in charge.

If you were wandering through a field and found a buried treasure of greater worth than you could imagine, you would try to buy that field. You would sell everything you own just to purchase it, because nothing you own compares to the wealth you would acquire. Love is that treasure.

Our Part:

Use *Humility* to acknowledge your need for Love and surrender everything you are and have to Spirit's control. Have a talk with Spirit where you admit so much of your actions and words have lacked love. And invite Love to take the driver's seat of your life. Invite Spirit to teach you, guide you and deliver you from the enemies of *Fear, Shame, and Arrogance.* Then listen to what Spirit says to you through your conscience. Every day commit to listening to Love through your conscience and any other ways Spirit wants to speak to you. Resolve to not grieve Spirit by doing or saying what you know is not loving. And, when you blow it, make amends to people, and thank Spirit for helping you notice the mistake and bringing out the best in you.

Use Humility to Increase Faith in Love

In our day and age, we seem to be consumed with whatever we take pleasure in. Historically, I have been a huge sports fan. I had all the sports apps, knew all the scores and stats of almost every sport in North America, and watched many, many live games. In fact, my emotions were tied to the team I cheered for. If my team won, I would be in a good mood all day. If they lost, I would be depressed and in a foul mood for a while. My emotions were tied to a team, and none of the players even knew I existed!

People treat their favourite TV shows similarly. Those with fifteen minutes of fame from starring in a reality series get adored or hated. Sometimes they even get death threats. Movie, music, and social media stars experience the same, as well as politicians and wealthy businesspeople.

We put our *Faith* in the famous among us. Whoever we admire and are entertained or inspired by is who we pay attention to, obsess over, listen to, and follow. If those folks live in a way that we agree with, we heap praise on them and hope to be like them. But if they act in a way that disappoints our expectations of them, we turn on them quickly. It's as if they have betrayed our trust and destroyed the *faith* we have put in them.

If we're going to be transformed by Love to live our best lives and walk in the truth of our value and design, then we need to direct our attention and *faith* towards Love. If we're filling our ears, eyes, and mind with more of news media, social media, and Hollywood than we are with the light and truth of Love, then our anxiety and depression are self-inflicted.

I recently deleted all my news, sports, and social media apps. I stopped watching sports on TV and I now am very picky with the few TV shows or movies I watch. They must be in line with the values of Spirit, or I won't spend time watching them. I chose to rid myself of any potential agents of *Fear, Shame, and Arrogance.* I'm reading a lot more and just talking with Spirit a lot. It's changed my life. I'm more able to access the peaceful, kind, and thoughtful components of my nature. Who you pay attention to is who you hear. As my dad used to say, "Show me your friends and I'll tell you who you are."

Our Part:

Invite Love to give you a heightened awareness of their presence in your life. Pay more attention to Spirit than to the world in your time and entertainment choices. Put your *faith* in Love. Think back to all the times in world history, and read stories, where Love made a difference in turning people's lives around. Investigate online how Spirit is currently making a difference in other people's lives. You'll get encouraged by realizing you're not alone in your quest to find and live for Love. Set your hopes and dreams on Love's unchanging nature. Love is real and they have made a real difference in the world.

As mentioned, *Humility* is the combination of *Honesty* and *Honour*. Each of these elements has a tool to enable us to get along with anyone, avoid offenses, receive what others have to offer, and build incredible relationships. Let's look at the *tools* of *Humility*.

Use Humility to Be Honest with Ourselves

I doubt anyone has ever improved on the ethic, "Love your neighbour as you love yourself." But to do that implies we need to love ourselves first. Sadly, that self-love is in short supply these days. People all over the world are deliberately hurting and killing themselves for lack of Love and the Joy and Hope Spirit brings. That is partly because we have lost sight of the *Honesty of Love.*

Honesty means a clear acknowledgement of what we're capable of, both good and bad. When it comes to how we motivate ourselves to give good to others, that's when we focus on the good that we're capable of. It's true that we are all capable of kindness, generosity, thoughtfulness, gentleness, and a host of other wonderful traits too numerous to mention here.

Speaking the Honesty of Love to ourselves daily is not optional. It is essential for growing *self-love*, and that is vital for enabling Love to flow through us.

When we speak the *Honesty of Love* to ourselves, we are showing complete authenticity. We are being real with ourselves and others. When we say what we are capable of, both good and bad, without comparisons, we are reconnected with the *Honesty of Love* that has the power to set us free from the lies of the enemies.

Notice I said we're *capable* of good traits. For the sake of avoiding the enemy of *Pride*, who promotes comparisons, that word *capable* is crucial. If I say something like, "I am kind," I could also ask, "Compared to who?" If positive affirmations are comparative in nature, they play into the hands of *Pride* and are ultimately destructive to Love flowing through us. Another trick of the enemies.

People always say, "Watch where you're going." That's because we usually end up where we're looking with our physical eyes. The same can be said about our mind's eye. If we're speaking the truth of the good we're capable of all day long, then that's what our mind will be focused on and that's where we'll end up. If we're saying to ourselves, "I'm capable of being patient today" throughout the day, then we're going to be focused on summoning patience. And, when we're impatient, we're going to notice it more readily and correct it.

The *Honesty* of *Humility* doesn't require a comparison. Remember, the truth sets us free from our enemies to flow in the freedom of Love. Speaking the truth of Love is honesty about our positive capabilities. That focus enables our best selves to emerge. If we're constantly looking at the good that we're capable of, we're more likely to give that good to others. That doesn't mean we deny the bad we're capable of. In fact, that has its usefulness in revitalizing our relationships too.

Use the Humility to Be Honest with Others

When it comes to what we expect or think we deserve from others, that's when we speak the truth of the bad that we're capable of. We are all capable of being selfish, rude, vindictive, hurtful, and jealous. The horrible parts of us don't deserve anything good from anyone else. Those parts don't deserve respect, kindness, generosity, or encouragement. So, when we get good from others, if we see it as a *Grace* gift we didn't deserve, we will be thankful. And, when we get bad from others, we can acknowledge the bad parts of us didn't deserve better. That helps us overlook or avoid offenses from anyone.

Someone might object on the basis that willingly receiving bad from others lacks boundaries. They may suggest we need to stand up for ourselves and put that person in their place out of self-respect. But is that the true wisdom of Love, or another false solution of *Fear*?

When a person knows and lives out how valuable and loveable they are, that affects how they treat others. Daily walking in the knowledge of our worth translates to treating others with the same worth. So, if a person is not treating us in loving ways, that must mean they are disconnected from the truth of Love that they are incredibly valuable and loveable.

Fear's answer to that problem is, "Make sure they know how valuable and loveable *YOU* are." Fear tells us in those moments to set boundaries that don't let that person in. Or Fear says to put that person in their place through a lecture or separation. But in the history of someone being mean to another person, no one has ever realized their worth by receiving a lecture or being abandoned!

Love's answer to that problem is very different. Spirit leads us to ask the question, "What can I do or say in this interaction to help that person connect with the truth of how valuable and loveable *THEY* are?" Fear wants us to retreat in self-protection.

Love wants us to advance in selfless service. Spirit wants everyone to unite with Truth and each other.

The nature of our relationship with that person affects the answer to Love's question. To a stranger or chronic abuser, the answer may be that I need to welcome them to discover their worth through someone else. To a neighbour or co-worker, the answer might be that I need to ask them if they're OK and show a genuine interest in the reasons behind their meanness to me in that exchange. To a close friend, partner, or family member, the answer might require a whole lot more effort and personal change. It's an easy question to ask, but a very difficult one to answer sometimes. That's how we know it's from Love, not Fear...it requires sacrifice to answer.

It's no wonder *Fear, Shame, and Arrogance* desire to disconnect us from the Truth of Love about who we are and why we're here. They cloud our judgment of ourselves with lies and doubt, spurring these on through comparisons and complaints. Their intent is to separate us from the Truth of Love, so we are weak, powerless, and alone. They accomplish this by attacking the way we think. We need to take back the ground of our mind.

Make no mistake, our mind is the battleground between Love and their enemies. It's no surprise mental health is under attack right now. Both Love and *Fear* and *Pride* know whoever controls the mind wins the battle. That's why we must take captive every thought to make it obedient to the Truth of Love. We are transformed by the renewing of our minds. And whatever we are speaking about is what we are thinking of. So, speak the truth of Love to yourself every day and avoid speaking the comparative complaints of the enemies. And watch love, peace, joy, and hope be restored to your soul.

Our Part:

Write at the top of a blank piece of paper "I'm thankful I'm capable of," and then fill the page with positive traits you are capable of. Put the paper in a prominent place where you'll see it every morning. At the start of each day, look at the list, considering your schedule, and note all the positive traits you're going to need that day for the people you meet and circumstances you'll encounter. Then start saying out loud that you're thankful you're capable of showing those traits today. Every time the circumstances of your day change—you get in the car to go somewhere, or you are going to speak to someone different—Speak the Truth of Love to yourself of the good you're capable of. Remember, what you focus on is where you end up.

Also, at the start of your day, and when your environment changes, say to yourself out loud, "Because I'm capable of being horrible today, I don't expect nor deserve anything good from anyone. When I get good, I will acknowledge it as a grace gift and be thankful. When I get bad from others or life, I will tell myself the bad parts of me didn't deserve better, and I relinquish my right to be offended." This will help you avoid offenses that lead to comparative complaints about not being or having enough. Above all, surrender your mind to Love every day.

Use Humility to Promote the Honour and Power of Love

I once saw a speaker try to demonstrate the principle of *honour* to a group of couples. He went to the back of the stage and brought out a tattered-looking violin. It was broken at the neck and hanging by the strings. It had scratch marks all over it and some wood was chipped off. He asked the audience what they would do with such an instrument if they found it in their attic. Each of them suggested they would throw it away. They said it's a piece of junk and can't be fixed to play as it was designed. The speaker acknowledged the wisdom of their decision based on the violin's appearance. Then he said, "But what if I read you the inscription on the inside of this violin. It says 'Stradivarius—1686'" and the audience audibly gasped. Then they realized why there were armed guards at the back. This was a very rare original violin created by a master. When he inquired of the audience what they would do with it now, they all suggested things like storing it in a vault or putting it in a museum. Now they were ready to honour the violin due to its rarity and origin.

As mentioned previously, our value as humans lies in the uniqueness of our design, purpose, and designer. Each of us is special because there's no one else designed like you. No one else is living your story. And you were designed by the one who IS Love. Everyone in your life deserves a *gasp of honour*!

There is great power in Love. The power of Love is enabled by unity, which can only be accomplished through mutual honour. Mutual honour is demonstrated in our attitude and actions. The attitude of honour comes by viewing everyone we meet as a funnel of Love. Everyone should be seen as the embodiment of Love because at some point Love designed us, can dwell in us, and flows through us.

Years ago, there was a campaign called WWJD or "What Would Jesus Do." While I applaud the effort to get everyone to behave well, I think the campaign was a bit misguided. Jesus is certainly a great person to emulate, but he never intended to make us all versions of himself. In fact, he may just be Love in human form who made us to be the best versions of ourselves.

If we want to use Jesus as an example, there's a much better story he told us to consider. It's written in the gospels that Jesus said that when he was hungry, we didn't feed him. When he was thirsty, we didn't give him a drink. And, when he was in need, we didn't help him. We will ask when that happened and he will say, "In as much as you've done to the least brothers of mine, you did it to me." The question he wants us to ask is not what he would do. The question is, "If everyone you saw was Jesus—the embodiment of Love—how would you treat them?" I believe we'd show people a lot more care.

With this view of others, we can use Humility to Honour Love in others. We do this by seeing everyone we meet as equally valuable funnels through which Love flows. This person you are meeting up with today is the one Love wants to bless through you. This person you're encountering today is the one Spirit wants to bless you through. This person you are with today has unique gifts, experiences, and insights you could benefit from. You have unique gifts, experiences, and insights they could benefit from. Whether it's from a lighthearted joke or a penetrating question, Love can, and wants, to flow through each of us for the benefit of others.

If Love is not flowing through one or both parties, it's only because the enemies—*Fear, Shame, and Arrogance*—are clogging up the flow. If the other person you are interacting with isn't loving, then they have lost sight of the nature of Love, and lost touch with the reality of who they are and why they're here. If they knew those three things, they would be loving. That person is not the problem, and neither are you. Enemies are the problem.

There is no need for you to be an agent of Fear or Arrogance or Shame. No one has ever connected with the Truth of how valuable and loveable they are through a lecture, putdown, or hard isolating boundary. We may be each other's sole source of soul water today. It's not wise to go crawling through the desert ignoring or attacking the only one who may have water! Honour people with the value they deserve and help them figure out the Truth of Love in their own way and timeframe. You can only control your part of mutual honour that leads to unity, and the power of Love.

Our Part:

Whenever you are interacting with someone remind yourself ahead of time, they are a funnel of Love and so are you. Spirit wants to flow through them to you and vice versa. If Love isn't flowing, then the enemies are at work. Summon compassion and patience for the other person, who may be under attack from Fear, Arrogance, or Shame.

If you witnessed someone who was under attack by a bully and was clearly helpless to defend themselves, wouldn't you spring into action to help them? Those being unkind, unloving, impatient, or rude to us are under attack from unseen enemies. We may not be able to defeat those enemies for them, but we can certainly react in ways to help that person tune out their enemies, if even for a moment, during our interaction.

In every conversation, especially with those we're closest to, and especially in conflict situations, ask yourself this question:

What can I do or say to connect this person with the truth of how valuable and loveable they are. That's the only question we need to ask to make the relationship better. It's a simple question to ask, but it's a very difficult question to answer. The answer may require we give in to what the other person wants but we don't. It may require we humble ourselves and apologize or let that person have the last word. And it may require we keep our mouths shut. Whatever the answer, the question is at the heart of Love and needs to be a part of our thought routine. Don't worry about what you get in return. Trust these principles of Love: You always get what you give, and you can't outgive Spirit! But we should spend our lives trying.

The Flow of Love That's Entered through Humility

Thankful Affirmations...

This is a declaration of appreciation for who Love made us to be and what they made us to do. Saying our authentic identity and purpose on a daily basis, or Speaking the Truth of Love, gives a voice to a thankful heart which positions us to see increase. When "Not Enough" is immersed in thankfulness—it turns to "more than enough." We don't need to change the "noughness" of life. We just need to alter our perspective of it through thankful affirmations. This combats the enemy of Fear, whose language is complaining.

LEADS TO...

Joy. This is a conscious awareness of Love's devotion to us. Spirit's Joy in us gives us the strength of encouragement and that...

SPURS US ON TO...

Hope. This is a Joyful anticipation of the good Love has for us. Which...

EMBOLDENS...

Faith. This is an assurance of Hope in Love's designs for us. And this is...

STRENGTHENED BY...

Attuning. This is where we turn our attention to Spirit's message about who we are and why we're here. And we tune out the world's messages to us that contradict the Truth of Love. Which...

LEADS BACK TO...Thankful Affirmations

This is the essential flow of Love we need to enter every day. (Notice how we can flow both ways.) It is entered by using Humility to Surrender to Spirit. But the flow can be interrupted by Love's enemies every day too. They usually do this at the point of attuning and faith, by distracting, and sewing doubt in our minds. That is why we must stay vigilant about what we allow in our mind through our eyes, ears, and concentration. But take heart, we get to do battle alongside one who never loses in the end. We only do battle on days that are called "Today," and there's only one of those. Plus, Love brings incredible bounty into our lives with each victory.

SECTION FOUR: The Results of Reconnection with Love

Chapter 8: Love Inspires Balanced Growth

Once we Reconnect with Love through Healing and Humility, it's as if Spirit welcomes us into the Realm of Love with a banquet. During the feast, the Master of Ceremonies opens our inner eyes to see the beauty, vastness, power, and freedom of the realm we will never be banished from. We realize daily that we get to stay Connected with Love as we experience all the wealth of the Realm.

Then Love shows us the gardens in the Realm. It's obvious as we roam that the King of the Realm of Love takes the greatest pride in his gardens. Spirit can hardly wait each day to walk through the gardens. It's as though Spirit treats gardens as a bride. Every time Love enters a garden is a consummation of marriage.

Then Love tells us of the great sacrifices made to bring each garden back from the brink of decay and death. Though created for beauty and rest, an enemy got in and sowed weeds that choked the life out of each garden. But Spirit spared no expense to redeem each garden and spends every day restoring glory according to Spirit's design. Then they reveal to us, we are Love's gardens.

The *Funnels* are *gardens*. Love is the owner. The *Truth of Love* is the gardener. And the *Spirit of Love* is the wind in the fields bringing all growth into shape. We are the pride and joy of Love's creation. We are the apple of their eye. We are the ones Spirit sacrificed everything for. And we who surrender to Love are being molded back into our original design.

With Love in charge of this realm and our lives, there is no danger, no hopelessness, and no striving to fill a void. There is no confusion, exhaustion, anxiety, or depression as we walk with

Spirit in Love's empire. There's either blessings or lessons that are guided by Spirit for our good. The enemies are forced to watch as we feast on the nutrients of the empire and grow.

The fruit that Love grows in us is peace, joy, patience, goodness, kindness, gentleness, meekness, self-control, and above all, love. This fruit blesses our Mental Health and Relationships. Turning our attention, and aligning our will, to Spirit's daily horticulture increases our thankfulness, joy, and peace. As days pass, the faithfulness, goodness, and consistency of Love increases faith and hope. Spirit replaces our fear and pride-influenced thoughts and behaviours with Love-based ideas and attitudes. The result is a clean conscience and the diminishing of all that Shame previously choked our lives with.

The fruit is not only given for us to enjoy but to bless others with too. The more we hang out with Love the more others notice this fruit in our lives. The more they notice, the more they are drawn to Spirit as well. In history, those most influenced by Love have had the greatest lasting impact for Love. Jesus and Mother Teresa spring to mind.

But Love knows this new fruit can't be grown in old gardens. The old gardens have been too compromised by the enemies to handle the splendour of Love's new fruit. That's why replacement and development in each Funnel of Love is necessary. Surrender takes care of replacement of the funnels as we'll see in the *Spiritual* section of this chapter. However, when we're given entrance to the Realm of Love, we become partners with Spirit in the privilege of Spirit's work in two ways.

First, the lessons of Love are the fertilizer that grows the fruit. And lessons in the Empire of Love are in opposite order of our earthly world. In the Realm of Love, the test comes before the lessons. Spirit allows a test in our lives and then shows us the lesson we're supposed to learn that leads to growth of more fruit.

Our partnership is to keep our eyes on Love during the test and have faith that the big picture is personal growth. That will lead to a greater flow of Love through our garden. As the saying goes, "Consider it pure joy whenever you face trials of many kinds because you know the testing of your life of faith leads to perseverance and perseverance builds character." It's not easy to be happy when troubles strike. But if we keep our eyes on Spirit during the tests, we know everything will be OK, as the life-blessing fruit is growing.

The tests Love lets into our lives are not pass/fail deals. They're just markers to let us know where we are on our journey and how much further we must go. Think of them as Spirit giving us our soul GPS location and directions of how to get where we want to be. Stress doesn't hurt so bad when we know it's leading us to a good place. If nothing else, trials make us more useful to those who are going through similar struggles by building the empathy of Love.

The point Spirit wants us to realize is when we struggle there's nothing wrong with us or them. We struggle because so much of the world is under the influence of Love's enemies. Many of the human funnels of Love are clogged up and Spirit is neither flowing in nor flowing out. The fruit is not evident in their lives. Our primary concern cannot be to criticize or judge the other funnels because they're not where we are, or don't have what we have. Ironically, that plays into the hands of the enemies and winds up clogging us too!

Spirit doesn't stop the suffering, because it's the nature of Love to *give* choices, not take them away. When we funnels choose to run with Love's enemies, they must let us go, or they wouldn't be Love anymore. But Spirit never worries about us because Love is the perfect gardener. For those of us Reconnected with Love, the privilege is to partner with Spirit by first enjoying the growth they bring.

The second way we partner with Love for growth is by making plans for development. As we've seen, Spirit wants us to experience growth. In fact, Love designed us with a need for development. From the beginning, we humans have sought achievement in agriculture, inventions, building, and exploration. We have sought to expand our family lines, the population, cities, knowledge, wisdom, and revelation. We have developed communication, modes of transportation, industry, and technology. Sometimes our enemies have motivated such growth, as in the case of wars. Other times, Spirit has been behind our desires, as in the case of family. Whatever the motivation, it is undeniable that our design includes a desire to advance as groups and individuals.

Ambition for more is our Love-given design. But that ambition for more must be rooted in the contentment Spirit brings after Healing and Humility. When we move forward in contentment, we're not trying to make up for something that's missing. We're just building out of love, which is rewarding for all involved, both givers and recipients. Desire that is surrendered to, and under the control of Love, is a never-ending joy that leads to ultimate fulfillment.

Desire that is still in the hands of Fear, Arrogance, or Shame always leads to destruction. When ambition is affected by our enemies, it is rooted in discontentment, and that leads to striving to obtain worth rather than revealing the truth of our intrinsic value. When we strive for more to make up for what is missing, more is never enough. It's as though we climb a ladder of success and reach the top only to discover we placed our ladder against the wrong building! Then we are back to Fear and Shame's thoughts and feelings. Misguided desires open us up to further attacks by our enemies. We can see this principle evident in addictive thinking and behaviour.

There are two rationales to our need to partner with Love to set goals for growth in all areas of our lives. The first reason is seen through an old saying that goes, "Without a vision people perish." I take that to mean, without something to look forward to, we experience an inner death. We get anxious, bored, or depressed when we're not moving in the direction of a desired outcome. We can see this when it comes to a holiday. Part of the joy of a trip is the planning. Much of the joy of Christmas is the anticipation. We need something desirable ahead for our mind to focus on. It helps if what lies ahead is new, mysterious, and represents positive change.

The second reason for setting goals with Love is that change is a part of life. We can name all kinds of things that change on a regular basis. Our age, the weather, our clothes, our living quarters, our families, a woman's mind (sorry, couldn't resist). Many things change daily, weekly, monthly, or yearly. It is undeniable that change is a part of life. The problem is, we humans don't always like, or adapt well, to change.

We like our "comfort zones." We wake up at the same time, have the same shower routine, take the same route to work every day, and eat the same meals every week. At work we are likely to sit in the same place in the staff room. If we go to church, we probably sit in the same pew every week. (I once got chastised at church for sitting in someone's spot! I literally had to shuffle down to make her happy.) When I lived in China, if I wanted to meet foreigners I'd go to McDonald's or KFC because that was familiar territory where expats were likely to frequent for a taste of their home comfort zone.

Comfort zones offer us a bit of security. It's as if the brain says, "You know, I did this before, and everything went OK. I think I should do it again...and again...and again, just to be safe." There is no change in a comfort zone. And therein lies a problem. If life equals change and we like things to stay the same for our sense of security, how do we navigate that dichotomy without frustration?

I find the difference between when I like change and when I don't is...who is in charge of the change? If I get to work and my boss changed my whole job description without talking to me first, I'm probably not going to react well. If I come home and my partner has changed her hair, the furniture, or the colour of the walls, without discussing it with me first, I'm not likely to appreciate that. However, if I change something I probably like that because I changed it for a reason.

The secret to navigating life's changes in the Realm of Love is to partner with Love to *be in charge of changes.* If we're surrendered and walking with Love, we can trust Spirit to make our plans lead to growth. If our plans don't line up with Love's plan, then they will bring us back on track at some point. There's no danger with Love in charge! There's only growth. But if we're not surrendered to Love, and still influenced by the *enemies*, we'll either be targets for *Fear* and *Pride's* attacks via other people, or our plans will leave us unfulfilled.

Love Plans to Grow Fruit in Our Lives in Seven Key Areas

Physical. Love gave us a body to manage. It is a house for our soul and the Spirit of Love to reside. It is a vehicle we live in until our soul and Spirit reach our final destination. And this vehicle starts deteriorating the moment it leaves the lot! The best we can do with it is sing with Carrie Underwood, "Jesus, take the wheel."

I jest. But care of the body is important because it's something Love, and the enemies, fight for control over. Any gift given to us by Spirit is incredibly valuable and something the enemies want to destroy. And people under the control of Fear, Shame, and Arrogance are either destroying, undermining, or inflating the value of their bodies. From addictions to obesity to pornography, the body has become out of line with Love's design.

Spirit wants it back. Love wants our body to be a physical sign of our Connection with Spirit. The body surrendered to Love is well-exercised, fed, and rested in balance. It doesn't have to be perfect, but Love desires our body to be taken care of as the gift it is. Comparing our body to anyone else's, feeding our body when it isn't hungry, resting our body when it isn't tired, or longing for someone else's body without Spirit at the centre of a committed relationship, represent the influence of Fear, Shame, and Arrogance. Give your body back to Love and listen to how they want you to manage it.

Intellectual. The body has a brain in it, and that needs to be stimulated. All through life we need to be feeding and challenging our minds. Spirit designed the brain to feel refreshed by new information, skill development, and the application of knowledge in wisdom. A mind connected with Love longs for nuggets of truth to feed on. When Spirit oversees our minds, it can't get enough insights for living.

Just remember, the mind is the battleground where wars are waged. On the one side, our enemies want to flash thoughts of Fear, Shame, and Arrogance into our mind. They wish for us to be consumed with comparisons and complaints, so we think we are not enough, don't know enough, aren't good enough, or are better than others. They want our thoughts to lead to selfishness, self-centredness, and self-loathing. They know if we entertain their thoughts we will be disconnected from the Truth of the nature of Love. We'll lose sight of who we are and why we're here. They know if we're disconnected from the thoughts of Love, we will gladly pick up their false tools to fix the real problem.

We must stay connected with the Truth of Love in our mind to keep experiencing all the Empire of Love has to offer. We stay connected by speaking the Truth of Love out loud every day. Whatever is coming out of our mouth is what our brain is focused on. We stay connected by replacing the sources of enemy messages with the sources of Spirit messages. We stay connected by thinking of the ways of collaboration rather than competition. We stay connected by delighting our mind in the ways of Love throughout the day.

Emotional. It's important to know why Love designed us with feelings, instead of like Vulcans. It's important to know what purpose emotions are supposed to have in Spirit's creation. And it's important to figure out how to release our Love-given emotions at the right times, to the right people, in the right ways.

Spirit designed a great communication system of the soul. The soul has needs built in because Love's purpose for our lives is relational. It's only in the context of healthy relationships that we get our needs of Security, Significance, and Service met. So, the needs propel us to relationships. When we're in relationships, the soul sends messengers to tell us whether we're getting our needs met or not. Those messengers are emotions.

If we're happy, peaceful, content, or any other host of feelings we like, that's the soul's way of saying, "Hey, we're getting all our needs met." When we figure out what the needs are that are being met, through the alert of our feelings, then we can get more of those needs.

If we're sad, angry, lonely, bitter, or any other host of feelings we don't like, that's the soul's way of saying, "Hey, we've got some needs that aren't getting met." When we figure out what needs are not being met, through the alert of our emotions, then we can get those needs by ourselves or from those we're in relationships with. When the needs of the soul are met, it stops sending the negative emotion messengers and starts sending the positive messengers.

One of the problems is, when we're disconnected from Love and under the influence of Fear, Shame, and Arrogance, we try to get rid of feelings without first listening to what they're trying to tell us about our needs. If we chase undesired emotions away with things like drinking, smoking, drug use, overeating, overworking, sex, or pornography, we ignore our needs. So, after the effects of those coping strategies have worn off, the soul will keep sending the same feelings to alert us to unmet needs. Making this a pattern of our lives is at the root of addictive thinking and behaviour.

A second problem with chasing our feelings away through unhealthy coping strategies is we empower the enemies. If emotions are messengers that reveal needs, then minimizing feelings devalues needs. For example, let's say you're in a conflict with your partner. When you express your feelings, if that person minimizes your feelings in any way, it sends you a devaluing message. We may subconsciously think, "Oh, if this person doesn't care about my feelings, then they don't care about my needs. If they don't care about my needs, they're not going to meet my needs. If they're not going to meet my needs, I can't trust them. If I can't trust them, why am I in a relationship with them?"

Minimizing feelings is devaluing and strengthens Shame. Shame can now say, "See, I told you you're not that valuable." Now imagine the person you're in a relationship with is YOU. If you chase your feelings away with substance abuse or any other coping strategy, you're saying to your own soul, your feelings are not important. You're telling your own soul you don't care about its needs. If you're doing that, is it any wonder your mental health and relationships are unhealthy?

Reconnecting with Love does not automatically make us emotionally mature. We may languish as emotional infants, children, or adolescents for years. But Love leads us down a path towards adulthood. That path is often wrought with pain, suffering, and difficult decisions. When we focus on the pain, we lose sight of Love. Yet Love is always there waiting, encouraging, and spurring us on towards emotional maturity. Emotional growth was always supposed to be a partnership between us and Love. The emotional pain of our past, combined with Spirit's perspective, has healing properties for us and others.

Social. Love is a relationship. Spirit made us relational, as evidenced by building us with needs that can only be met in the context of relationships. Love makes relationships fun and rewarding. So, if we're isolated or anxious about being with people, there's a good chance we've become distanced from Love in our social life. Let's look at two main reasons this can happen before addressing how to fix it.

When people hurt us, they become Agents of Fear, Shame, or Arrogance. As such we may deem them as bad, mean, selfish, or evil in some way. Then we tend to relate to them out of Fear, Shame, or Arrogance. We shut down to them, label them, blame them, or hurt them back. Relating in such ways makes us agents of the enemies in the other person's life. So, guess what they do back to us? It is a vicious cycle the enemies gladly promote. If this pattern has been repeated over and over in someone's life, is it any wonder they have a small circle of friends, or none at all?

When such interactions are left unresolved or unhealed, resentments can easily turn to bitterness. And bitterness always opens us up to attacks from the enemies. By harbouring past emotional pain, we set ourselves up as a judge. The basis for our judgements is comparisons to US. We tell ourselves we would never act or treat someone like they did to us or those we take up offenses for.

One problem with living as judges of others is we all have blind spots. Isn't it true that today you know or see something about yourself you didn't see five years ago? You couldn't have known what you'd be like as a married person before you got married. You couldn't have known what you'd be like as a parent until you had children. Life changes, reveals, and makes us who we are. That's not always a good thing. With that in mind, isn't it also possible that five years from now you will know or see something about yourself you don't know or see today? Isn't it also possible those we are judging may have gone through something we couldn't possibly know about through insight or experience? So, we couldn't possibly know what we would do if we were in their shoes. Then how can we trust our judgements of others today?

To breathe life into our motivation for socialization, and rid ourselves of anxiety, we must stop listening to the lies of Fear and Pride. We must give up our right to judge anyone. We must keep our attention on the Truth of Love, that no one—regardless of how they treat us—can diminish our value and lovability. And that we are here to be funnels and agents of Love.

Purpose. One of the great ironies of life is that the less we think of ourselves, the better we feel about ourselves. I think Mother Teresa went to bed every night feeling great about herself. Because all day long she was thinking of others and how to help them. We see this principle evident in our own lives when we give someone a gift just because we care. When they receive it with thankfulness it brings joy to our hearts. That reveals both the Nature of Love and our design.

Love designed us to help others and they will lead us to prepared opportunities to help others. For those reconnected with Love, the desire to help is the manifestation of the connection and attention to Spirit. And since the system Spirit set up involves reaping what we sow, the results of helping others in Love is receiving more help from others in Love. Pretty good system I'd say.

The only thing is, helping others must be in line with the motivational gifts Love designed us with. Trying to help others in ways we're not gifted in or passionate about is like trying to take a Ferrari mudbogging. It's never going to go well. But fulfilling our purpose when it's in line with our gifts is like taking a Ferrari on the racetrack. That's where we want to be. We'll take a closer look at the possible gifts Spirit made us with in the next chapter. For now, it's enough to realize that living in the Realm of Love involves meaningful, creative, fulfilling service.

Spiritual. We are all spiritual beings with a body. The spirit under the influence of the enemies dies. There is no life in Fear, Shame, and Arrogance. These enemies only steal, destroy, and kill the life in us. Love is the only one who can restore our spiritual life. Because Love is *a* Spirit and Love is *the* Spirit of Life.

When we use Spirit's tool—humility—to heal, find and speak the truth, and reconnect, Love gives us a new Spirit. This new Spirit cannot be stolen, destroyed, or killed by the enemies. Because this new Spirit IS Love. When we surrender, Spirit comes into the house that is us and resides. And Love NEVER leaves. But don't worry, Spirit isn't like other houseguests...you don't want Love to leave!

Wherever Spirit lives improves the house and the neighbourhood. Love in us increases our peace, joy, love, hope, gentleness, kindness, generosity, faithfulness, and willingness to forgive others. Spirit does this through a lot of creative ways. Sometimes they lead us to gather with a community of like-minded people to increase Love's fruit. Other times they use our time in nature to refresh our Spirit. Sometimes Love utilizes the stories we read or watch to inspire us spiritually. And there's also moments of quiet meditative reflection that attune us to Spirit's presence.

Whatever the means, we need to prioritize such spiritual moments and activities to have a heightened awareness of Love's presence, power, and purpose in our lives. One of the privileges and pleasures of living in the Realm of Love is spending time with the King. We invite Love's presence by daily giving Spirit the authority to rule and reign over our bodies, minds, and hearts. We do that through surrender and submission. The King wants friends and family, but we can't get adopted as such without recognizing Love as the King.

Resource Management. Love gives us three main resources in life to manage—*Time, Energy and Possessions.* Managing these three areas well, with integrity, is important to Spirit. Love knows if we're always in a hurry and never have enough time to get things done, we will feel gross about ourselves and life. They know if we don't have enough money to pay our bills, take nice holidays, give our children what they need growing up, and be able to rest in our old age with no worries, we will feel awful. Spirit also knows when we are overworked, tired all the time, and depleted of energy and motivation for life, we will feel dire about ourselves and life.

Love cares about our needs and practical dilemmas. That's why they give us knowledge and wisdom to manage such things with skill. Those Reconnected with Love, residing in the Realm of Love, have a natural inclination towards priorities and balance. Love tells us what's important if we're listening, so we can put first things first. They also let us know when we're becoming out of balance and when we might be buying in to the subtle lies of our enemies.

Remember, the enemies want us to believe we're missing something. They want us to think we're not enough, don't have enough, and aren't doing enough. They say, if we could just be more, have more, and do more, life would be better. Then we would feel *Secure* and *Significant*. So, the enemies promote striving after more in the few areas we gain success in, like work or our physical life. We then pour ourselves into one or two areas of the seven well areas, striving for fulfillment and success. We buy into the lies of the enemies who tell us we're doing the right thing. After all, we're striving for the health of our bodies, families, or future. But eventually, striving leads to frustration, burnout, or collapse, as we realize it's never enough. Nothing inspired by Fear, Shame, and Arrogance ever fulfills. Again, there's no life in the enemies.

To emphasize the importance of balance in all these seven areas of life, let's use a barrel as an analogy. We all know what a barrel looks like—it has wooden slats that go up and down with a brace around it. If we put a hose in the barrel, turn the tap on, and walk away, when is the water going to pour out of the barrel? Basic physics says the water will flow out when it reaches the top.

However, let's say someone took an axe to the barrel and they hacked away at the slats. Now one slat goes to the top, but another one is 75% up. One is 50% up. Another is 30% up and one is 10% up. If I pour water into this deformed barrel, when is the water going to pour out? Will it reach the top slat? Of course not. The water will start pouring out at the lowest slat and never get to a higher level.

In this analogy, water represents life, vitality, energy, excitement, joy, fulfillment, and peace that Love wants to fill our lives with. The slats represent the seven areas of our lives. We can only be as excited, fulfilled, and rewarded in life as our lowest area, not our highest.

Some people pour all their time and energy into one area, like work. They climb the ladder of success and achieve all they dream of. But at some point, they realize it's not enough. They're out of balance and not paying attention to some important areas of their lives. They grow restless, bored, anxious, or depressed because they're not growing in certain areas, and they've become disillusioned about their whole value system.

In the Realm of Love goal setting is about *giving* not *getting*. Our connection with the Truth of Love about our value and lovability, and our purpose for existing, lets us start setting goals from a strength's perspective. The attitude, while continuing to use humility, could be described as, "What can I offer my sphere of influence in these seven areas?" or "How can I let Love flow through me in new ways, in these seven areas?"

Love wants to fulfill every area of our lives. If every area of our lives is surrendered, Spirit will grow fruit that feeds us and those we care for. If we're out of balance or not growing, it's a sign we've lost our much-needed heightened awareness of Spirit's presence, power, and purpose in our lives.

Our Part:

Rate yourself on a scale of 1–10 in each of the seven areas. Think of what a perfect a ten would look like in each area and compare yourself to that. Whatever number you give yourself, think about what the next number or two up would look like. What would be different about your life if you were at that higher number? What would you have more of, or less of? Who would you have, or not have, in your life to promote that growth? Write all that down.

That next number up that you want to arrive at becomes your long-term vision or goal to reach for. Now think about the short-term steps that will be necessary for you to reach that number.

Those become your short-term goals. These goals should be specific and measurable.

One of the cool things about setting goals is we can usually use our strengths to build our weaknesses. For example, I'm strong in the physical area. I enjoy sports, being in shape, eating well and getting good rest. However, I'm weak in the social area. I'm an introvert, I move around a lot, and I now work from home.

So, I use my physical life to build my social life. I'm involved in team sports where I can get to know other people. I've also joined hiking groups, dance classes, and a pickleball league. When I go golfing, I'm always trying to connect with new people and exchange contact information. This way I'm doing something I enjoy while building something that doesn't come naturally to me.

This can work with other areas too. If we're good intellectually but not spiritually or emotionally, then we can start reading or watching talks on those weaker areas. If we're good socially but not emotionally or in resource management then those subjects can be the topics of our interactions at times to gain inspiration. It doesn't always work, but we can usually use our strengths to build our weaknesses. And we must build those weaknesses to gain balance. When we do, Love is there to whisper through our inner voice, "That was awesome. I love seeing you grow!" That's why it's important not to leave goals too vague or unmeasurable. We need to see results to be encouraged by Love.

If you lack motivation or insight as to how to grow, recruit someone you admire and trust as an accountability partner. When I've approached people and told them I respect them in a certain area and would like to become more like them, they have all reacted well. People are usually encouraged to be looked up to and are eager to help keep me motivated towards goal achievement. Because my goals are specific and measurable, it's easy for my partners to know what I'm trying to accomplish and then check in on me regularly for reports on my growth. And I know when I'm going to be asked and checked up on that I'll be more conscientious to strive towards my goals. It's a win-win-win as Love, me, and my partners get the encouragement of praise.

When setting goals, it's vital not to bite off more than we can chew. Many people stay away from goal setting because they don't want to set themselves up for failure and disappointment. But if we commit our plans to Love and then baby step ourselves towards positive change, we get a boost with every step. The consequences of not setting goals and not seeing growth are far worse than setting a goal and falling short. Try to always have at least two specific measurable goals in all seven areas. But focus more attention and energy on your lower areas.

The key is to stay connected with Love when goal setting. Knock on doors and invite Love to open or close them according to Love's plan. If two doors open simultaneously it may be a test from Love, or it may be a temptation from the enemies. Either way, we're trusting Love to bless or teach us. Both are useful in Love's plan for our growth!

Chapter 9: Love Revitalizes Our Motivational Gifts

To design something, we usually need a *blueprint*. Love's blueprint for our life is called *Motivational Gifts*. Every human being has certain motivational gifts that they are higher in than others, to alert them to their specific purpose in life. As the name implies, these gifts motivate us to help others in specific ways.

When someone's not connected to Love and doesn't live in the Realm of Love, they can still serve in line with their motivational gifts and accomplish some things. But unless we're reconnected with Love, there's no power in our efforts. Just like a disconnected hair dryer could probably dry hair if you waved it around fast enough. But plugging it in makes it more effective!

For Love to truly empower those in the Realm, we funnel gardens need to be working together with our motivational gifts. Let's use a hypothetical problem to illustrate this point.

Let's say there is a seniors' centre on one side of a busy highway and a mall on the other side. The seniors like going to the mall to pass the time. The problem is there is no close way to get across the busy highway to the mall. The crosswalks are too far for many seniors to navigate. If we gathered a group of people who had different motivational gifts, they would all try to solve this dilemma in a different way.

The *leaders* in the group may have called the meeting in the first place. They purposely gathered a variety of people and gifts to create a collaborative approach to solving the seniors' problem. And people probably attended the meeting due to the charismatic way the leaders communicated the need. At the meeting the leaders cast a vision of a solved problem—seniors going to the mall to connect with each other and have fun. Then the leaders invite an open dialogue to find a way to realize the vision.

Now the *administrators* in the group pipe up right away to draw everyone's attention to the meeting agenda they created after they were recruited by the leader. They make sure everyone understands the agenda and order of business. They tell how they've already alerted the city of the meeting and possible proposals that may come forth from the meeting. Then they go quiet again until the end of the meeting and take minutes along the way.

Those with gifts of *perception* speak next. They warn of the coming doom for the senior population if a solution isn't achieved soon. If anyone during the meeting minimizes the needs of seniors, these perceivers quickly step in to reveal blind spots and advocate for renewed commitment. It's clear to all that this group won't compromise in their efforts to arrive at the desired end.

The *teachers* in the crowd now come to the front of the meeting hall to outline all the possible solutions to the problem. They present well-researched information in an easy-to-understand style. They include charts, graphs, and illustrations of outcomes if each solution is adopted. When they give time for questions and answers, they stick to the facts without giving away their preferences.

At this point the *servers* tell the group they made cupcakes and punch for later and everyone is welcome to enjoy the treats after the meeting. They also mention they'd be happy to volunteer to walk seniors across the busy highway. Then they pass out napkins and dismiss themselves so they can set out the goodies.

Those with *compassion* gifts chime in at this point. They mention how they've been speaking to the seniors and how worried they are that this dilemma has caused a lot of grief. They already conducted a support meeting to hear out the seniors and ask what solutions they'd suggest. They brought Kleenex too, if anyone needs some.

When it's decided an overpass walkway should be built to help the seniors get safely across to the mall, the *givers* assure everyone they'll make sure enough funds are made available to complete the project. They then ask the administrators to help start a crowdfunding project.

As the meeting is winding down, the *encouragers* thank everyone for attending. They go on about how caring and loving everyone has been with their involvement. They thank the leaders for putting this meeting together. Then they make special mention of the servers who baked cupcakes.

Finally, the administrators write down everyone's email to send them a copy of the minutes and draw everyone's attention to how the meeting went overtime, and end with "but please do enjoy some cupcakes before you leave."

Every gift looks at the situation from a different perspective and finds a different way to help. All perspectives are welcomed and useful in the Realm of Love. The point is, we need each other. Remember, the power of Love is unity through mutual honour. If everyone had the same perspective and gift, that's not unity, that's *conformity*. Conformity lacks *diversity*. Without diversity there are limitations within the Empire of Love. Love has no limitations, so neither can Love's Realm.

In the Empire of Love, we funnel gardens are like a body. Every part of the body has a different function, but we all need each other. The eyes don't say to the ears, "We don't need you, we can see." The arm can't say to the leg, "I have no use for you, since I can reach things for myself." (The leg would be like, "Seriously, dude? How are you getting anywhere to reach anything?")

There is no isolating in the Realm of Love. There's no need or desire to isolate because the effects of fear are diminished. We're all being healed through using humility, so we're not fearfully waiting for the next crisis. We're not cynically anticipating rejection, judgement, or abandonment. And we're all equally valued and loved, so there's no use for competitions or comparisons. Within the Realm we members see each other like a family.

The parent of the family is Love. Our siblings are the Truth of Love and all the other funnel gardens of Love. And the Spirit of Love is what unites us all in the Realm. Since Unity is facilitated through diversity of gifts, it's important for each of us to identify which motivational gifts we have. So, let's take a closer look at each gift.

The following is a summary of each motivational gift, accompanied by a survey to determine if you might have this particular gift. There is no right or wrong, pass or fail, to these surveys. After taking them all and adding the strengths of each to the weaknesses, just note which ones you scored the highest in and those are likely your gifts.

TEACHER

Teachers have a Love-given capacity to serve Love by making the Truth of Love known with accuracy and simplicity. Teachers tend to have a strong temperament, are confident, not easily swayed, and are decisive. Take the survey to see if you are strong in this gift.

GIFT OF TEACHING

0 = Never	3 = Usually
1 = Seldom	4 = Mostly

2 = Sometimes 5 = Always

Characteristics:

1. Presents ideas in a logical, systematic way 0 1 2 3 4 5

2. Likes to validate ideas by intensive research 0 1 2 3 4 5

3. Likes to study and do research 0 1 2 3 4 5

4. Likes to study words and their precise meanings 0 1 2 3 4 5

5. Uses illustrations to validate ideas 0 1 2 3 4 5

6. Resists taking information out of context 0 1 2 3 4 5

7. More objective than subjective 0 1 2 3 4 5

8. Develops and uses a large vocabulary 0 1 2 3 4 5

9. Researches the sources of other teachers 0 1 2 3 4 5

10. Believes the gift of teaching is the most important 0 1 2 3 4 5

11. Prioritizes facts over opinions 0 1 2 3 4 5

12. Asks questions before accepting information 0 1 2 3 4 5

13. Emotionally self-controlled 0 1 2 3 4 5

14. Has only a select circle of close friends 0 1 2 3 4 5

15. Believes knowledge can affect change 0 1 2 3 4 5

Subtotal ________

Problems:

1. Tends to neglect the practical application of facts 0 1 2 3 4 5

2. Slow to accept viewpoints of others. Argumentative. 0 1 2 3 4 5

3. Tends to develop pride in study and learning 0 1 2 3 4 5

4. Lacks warmth in personality. Can be inflexible. 0 1 2 3 4 5

5. Easily sidetracked. Has unfinished projects. 0 1 2 3 4 5

Subtotal _________

(Add strengths to weaknesses. Do NOT subtract!)

Total _________

GIVER

Givers have a Love-given desire and capacity to meet practical needs through gifts. Those with this gift are often unaware of it, due to their high capacity to serve and teach. But they get particular joy in contributing to practical needs where they can see the results. Take the survey to see if you are high in this gift.

GIFT OF GIVING

0 = Never 3 = Usually

1 = Seldom 4 = Mostly
2 = Sometimes 5 = Always

Characteristics:

1. Gives freely of money, possessions, time, and energy 0 1 2 3 4 5

2. Likes to give quietly without others knowing it 0 1 2 3 4 5

3. Wants to feel part of the project they are giving to 0 1 2 3 4 5

4. Wants gifts to be of high quality or something handmade 0 1 2 3 4 5

5. Gives only when it's of free-will. Resists pressure giving. 0 1 2 3 4 5

6. Views hospitality as an opportunity to give 0 1 2 3 4 5

7. Handles their finances with wisdom and frugality 0 1 2 3 4 5

8. Quick to volunteer where a need arises 0 1 2 3 4 5

9. Depends on spouse to confirm the amount of gift 0 1 2 3 4 5

10. Industrious and conscientious. Tends towards success. 0 1 2 3 4 5

11. Wise with investments and business 0 1 2 3 4 5

12. Not gullible or easily duped 0 1 2 3 4 5

13. Possesses natural wisdom and accepts advice 0 1 2 3 4 5

14. Gives to support people and projects believed in 0 1 2 3 4 5

15. Keeps track of people and projects given to 0 1 2 3 4 5

Subtotal ______

Problems:

1. May desire to control the person or project given to 0 1 2 3 4 5

2. May pressure others to give 0 1 2 3 4 5

3. May upset family and friends with the pattern of giving 0 1 2 3 4 5

4. Has a tendency to spoil their own children 0 1 2 3 4 5

5. May use giving to get out of other responsibilities 0 1 2 3 4 5

Subtotal _______

Total ________

PERCEPTION

Those with the gift of perception have a Love-given capacity and desire to reveal the Truth of Love to others. They have a strong desire to help others connect with Love so that order is brought back to life. They are often forceful communicators who see issues as black and white. When they see people being affected by Fear, Shame, or Arrogance, they boldly speak up. While they see themselves as proclaimers of Truth with pure motives, others may perceive them as blunt or abrasive. Take the survey to see if this is your primary gift.

GIFT OF PERCEPTION

0 = Never
1 = Seldom
2 = Sometimes

3 = Usually
4 = Mostly
5 = Always

Characteristics:

1. Quickly identifies good and bad motives 0 1 2 3 4 5

2. Sees things as black and white. Uncompromising. 0 1 2 3 4 5

3. Perceives the character of groups 0 1 2 3 4 5

4. Perceives the character of individual people 0 1 2 3 4 5

5. Experiences and embraces brokenness in own life 0 1 2 3 4 5

6. Glad to see brokenness (humility) in others 0 1 2 3 4 5

7. Operates according to principles and integrity 0 1 2 3 4 5

8. Frank. Outspoken. Does not mince words. 0 1 2 3 4 5

9. Persuasive in method of speaking 0 1 2 3 4 5

10. Identifies with and grieves over the mistakes of others 0 1 2 3 4 5

11. Eager to help others see their blind spots and change 0 1 2 3 4 5

12. Feels the need to verbalize or dramatize what they see 0 1 2 3 4 5

13. Has strong opinions 0 1 2 3 4 5

14. Makes quick evaluations 0 1 2 3 4 5

15. Has strict personal standards 0 1 2 3 4 5

Subtotal _____

Problems:

1. Tends to be judgmental and blunt 0 1 2 3 4 5

2. Forgets to praise partial progress of others 0 1 2 3 4 5

3. Relentless in getting others to mature/change 0 1 2 3 4 5

4. Intolerant of opinions/views of those who differ 0 1 2 3 4 5

5. Has a few or no close friends 0 1 2 3 4 5

Subtotal _____

Total ______

LEADER & ADMINISTRATOR

These folks have a Love-given capacity and desire to serve Spirit by organizing, administrating, leading, and promoting the affairs of the Realm of Love. They are very comfortable telling others what to do. They have an ability to know who can do a job. They tend to be efficient, decisive, and self-sufficient. When healed and humble, they exhibit a lot of optimism. Take the survey to see if this is a gift you are strong in.

GIFTS OF LEADERSHIP & ADMINISTRATION

0 = Never	3 = Usually
1 = Seldom	4 = Mostly
2 = Sometimes	5 = Always

Characteristics:

1. Highly motivated to organize what they're responsible for 0 1 2 3 4 5

2. Likes to use graphs, charts, outlines, and diagrams 0 1 2 3 4 5

3. Prefers to be under authority in order to have authority 0 1 2 3 4 5

4. Waits for responsibility to be delegated to them by leader 0 1 2 3 4 5

5. Will assume responsibility if no structural leadership exists 0 1 2 3 4 5

6. Sees the overall picture and sets long-term goals 0 1 2 3 4 5

7. Visualizes the resources and people who can help 0 1 2 3 4 5

8. Enjoys delegating and supervising 0 1 2 3 4 5

9. Will endure criticism to accomplish tasks 0 1 2 3 4 5

10.Fulfilled to see everything fit together to accomplish goals 0 1 2 3 4 5

11. Willing to let others get the credit 0 1 2 3 4 5

12. Desires to finish strong, then move on to other projects 0 1 2 3 4 5

13. Has strong convictions. Usually a leader. 0 1 2 3 4 5

14. Wants to see tasks completed as soon as possible 0 1 2 3 4 5

15. Writes notes to self 0 1 2 3 4 5

Subtotal ____

Problems:

1. Upset when others don't share same convictions/goals 0 1 2 3 4 5

2. Becomes callous due to criticism 0 1 2 3 4 5

3. Less sensitive to personal needs of helpers 0 1 2 3 4 5

4. Tends to neglect personal and family needs due to goals 0 1 2 3 4 5

5. Workaholic, married to the job 0 1 2 3 4 5

Subtotal _____

Total ______

SERVERS

Servers have a Love-given capacity and desire to serve Love through practical help that meets physical, mental, emotional, and relational needs. Servers are quick to spring into action when they see a need. They give of themselves sacrificially without thought of the cost. They like to serve with their hands and appreciate order. Take the survey now to discover if you are a server.

GIFT OF SERVING

0 = Never	3 = Usually
1 = Seldom	4 = Mostly
2 = Sometimes	5 = Always

Characteristics:

1. Recognizes practical needs and quick to meet them 0 1 2 3 4 5

2. Especially enjoys manual projects 0 1 2 3 4 5

3. A detail person. Keeps meticulous house or office. 0 1 2 3 4 5

4. Remembers people's likes and dislikes 0 1 2 3 4 5

5. Enjoys being a host. Loves to serve guests. 0 1 2 3 4 5

6. Will stay with a project until it's accomplished 0 1 2 3 4 5

7. Has a hard time saying "No." Involved in many projects. 0 1 2 3 4 5

8. Meets others' needs before their own 0 1 2 3 4 5

9. Likes short-term gains over long-term goals 0 1 2 3 4 5

10. Grateful for sincere appreciation. Detects insincerity. 0 1 2 3 4 5

11. Does more than asked to do. Generous nature. 0 1 2 3 4 5

12. Has high energy level 0 1 2 3 4 5

13. Loyal 0 1 2 3 4 5

14. Prefers doing a job over delegating it 0 1 2 3 4 5

15. Supportive of others who are in leadership 0 1 2 3 4 5

Subtotal _____

Problems:

1. Critical of others who don't meet obvious needs 0 1 2 3 4 5

2. May neglect family needs in favour of others 0 1 2 3 4 5

3. May become pushy in eagerness to help 0 1 2 3 4 5

4. Hard to accept being served by others 0 1 2 3 4 5

5. Easily hurt when unappreciated by others 0 1 2 3 4 5

Subtotal _____

Total ______

ENCOURAGER

Encouragers have the Love-given capacity and desire to serve Love by motivating others to act. They accomplish this through validating current character and behaviour to inspire better character and behaviour. They recognize that people don't respond to critical lectures by asking for more advice. Encouragers notice the good they see and are usually approached for advice due to their unconditional acceptance. If you've got an encourager in your life, do not let them go! Take the survey now to see if this is your primary gift.

GIFT OF ENCOURAGEMENT

0 = Never	3 = Usually
1 = Seldom	4 = Mostly
2 = Sometimes	5 = Always

Characteristics:

1. Likes to teach others to live positively 0 1 2 3 4 5

2. Wants a visible response when teaching/speaking 0 1 2 3 4 5

3. Avoids information that lacks practical application 0 1 2 3 4 5

4. Likes practical steps to aid personal growth 0 1 2 3 4 5

5. Encourages others to develop their abilities 0 1 2 3 4 5

6. Likes to do personal counselling 0 1 2 3 4 5

7. Will discontinue counselling if no effort to change is seen 0 1 2 3 4 5

8. Dislikes teaching that lacks practical application 0 1 2 3 4 5

9. Views trials as opportunities to grow/mature 0 1 2 3 4 5

10. Accepts people as they are. Non-judgmental. 0 1 2 3 4 5

11. Loved by others due to positive attitude/outlook 0 1 2 3 4 5

12. Decisive 0 1 2 3 4 5

13. Finishes what is started 0 1 2 3 4 5

14. Quick to clear up problems with others when possible 0 1 2 3 4 5

15. Depends on partner as a sounding board 0 1 2 3 4 5

Subtotal ____

Problems:

1. Can interrupt others in eagerness to give advice 0 1 2 3 4 5

2. Uses information out of context to make a point 0 1 2 3 4 5

3. May be "cut and dried" in prescribing steps of action 0 1 2 3 4 5

4. Outspoken. Openly disagrees. Opinionated. 0 1 2 3 4 5

5. Can become overconfident and independent 0 1 2 3 4 5

Subtotal _____

Total _____

COMPASSION

Those with the compassion gift have a Love-given capacity and desire to serve Love through empathy and comforting those in distress. Compassionate people share the joys and sorrows of others. They are drawn to the sick, aged, and handicapped among us. They don't act out of pity as they see themselves as equals to those they help. You can frequently find them working with those who struggle with mental health and addictions. Answer the questions below to surmise if this is your gift.

GIFT OF COMPASSION

0 = Never	3 = Usually
1 = Seldom	4 = Mostly
2 = Sometimes	5 = Always

Characteristics:

1. Easily discerns the motives of others 0 1 2 3 4 5

2. Looks for the good in people. Non-critical. 0 1 2 3 4 5

3. Senses emotional atmosphere of group/person 0 1 2 3 4 5

4. Attracted to people who are hurting or in distress 0 1 2 3 4 5

5. Wants to remove hurts and relieve stress of others 0 1 2 3 4 5

6. More concerned with mental/emotional hurt than physical 0 1 2 3 4 5

7. Motivated to help people have healthy relationships 0 1 2 3 4 5

8. Careful with words and actions, not to offend 0 1 2 3 4 5

9. Drawn to others with same gift of compassion 0 1 2 3 4 5

10. Thoughtful. Loves to do things for others. 0 1 2 3 4 5

11. Trusting. Expects others to be honest and reliable. 0 1 2 3 4 5

12. Doesn't like to be rushed in a job or activity 0 1 2 3 4 5

13. Loves to see others happy. Grieves with hurting. 0 1 2 3 4 5

14. Good at non-verbal communication 0 1 2 3 4 5

15. Ruled by heart over head 0 1 2 3 4 5

Subtotal _____

Problems:

1. Tends to be indecisive 0 1 2 3 4 5

2. Tends to take up another's offense 0 1 2 3 4 5

3. Easily hurt by others 0 1 2 3 4 5

4. Can lack boundaries and take on other's emotions/issues 0 1 2 3 4 5

5. Compassion can be misinterpreted by opposite sex 0 1 2 3 4 5

Subtotal ____

Total _____

There are no *bad* motivational gifts. Serving Love with our primary motivational gifts feeds the soul. The soul that's being fed a healthy diet of motivational gift usage never gets full. However, trying to use your lower motivational gifts to serve can lead to bad outcomes. What I mean is, serving in capacities we're not passionate about, even though well-meaning, drains the soul and burns us out. The motivation dries up. When that happens, we may be giving a foothold for *Shame* to attack us because we may get down on ourselves over quitting a good thing. So, it's important to know what our gifts are and stick to the opportunities that utilize our gifts. Listening to Love helps sort this all out.

Chapter 10: Love Commissions Creative Service

Love is always at work. The work of Love is to *Create*. And when you're a child of Love, every day is "Take your kid to work day." We get to *co-create* with Love. In the Realm of Love, we are blessed with constant opportunities to use our motivational gifts to help all those whom Spirit brings into our lives. Spirit uses the lessons we've been taught, the hardships we've gone through, and the insights we've gained, to encourage and inspire others.

As I've hammered home by now, we are funnel gardens that are designed for Love to flow through. But if there's no outflow of Love, then there's no room for inflow. The outflow of Love is Creative Service.

One of the great ironies of Love's design is that *the less we think about ourselves, the better we feel about ourselves*. The more we're invested in helping others—being selfless instead of selfish—the more positive thoughts and feelings we have about ourselves. We can sense this when we give someone a gift. When they open it and respond to us with appreciation, it makes us feel warm inside. Or, doing random acts of kindness, such as holding doors open for people, shovelling the snow from someone's driveway for them, and any other way we give practical help to others throughout our week, give us great feelings about ourselves.

Remember the soul's great communication system? When the soul has a need that is met, it sends a messenger emotion to tell us we're getting something we need and to keep it up. One of the primary needs Love built us with—*soul water*—is *Service*. So, when Love leads us to serve, Love is meeting our need.

Spirit has already equipped us with motivational gifts to use as Spirit leads. And the creative service Love blesses us with utilizes those gifts. After we are finished meeting other people's needs, our needs are met too. The result is Spirit has increased our self-respect and supernaturally strengthened our mental health. Those blessed through our creative service are likely better off and have a soft predisposition towards us. So, the result is also supernaturally vitalized *relationships*.

This is why the most recent mental health mantra of "I just need to focus on myself" can be a false solution to a real problem. I understand the sentiment, but the application can take us in the opposite direction of where Love wants us to head. Part of "focusing on ourselves" needs to be prioritizing why Spirit has us here. That's about creative service that benefits others. If we want to boost our mental state, and change negative feelings to positive, then find someone worse off and create some way to serve them. Our problems fade away when we exert our energy, time, and expertise to help others.

Traits of Love That Inspire Creative Service:

Revelation

Revelation is a Word from Love. The foundation of our creative service must be Revelation. There are two types of *Revelation*—*Ancient* and *Current*. They are both *Alive* because the Word of Love is Life. We are made alive through Love's Word to us and in us.

The *Ancient Revelation* was written down by those previously reconnected with Love. Studying the Word of Love recorded for our training is as natural as going to school to get a degree for the field we want to dedicate our vocational lives to. It's more useful than going to YouTube these days to learn how to make omelettes or play piano.

No initiative, program, activity that Spirit inspires us to do in creative service will ever contradict Living Ancient Revelation. Wisdom doesn't need to change from generation to generation. However, the application of the Word of Love does change from age to age. That's why we need Current Revelation to inform us of modern ways to apply wisdom.

Too many people only know and rely on Ancient Revelation. It's usually the ones who made a big reconnection with Love, but don't do daily reconnections. It's as if their knowledge of Ancient Revelation has become a badge of honour for bragging rights. The knowledge was useful, but now it's become like a car air freshener that has no aroma left. It's become an ornament.

When we attune our attention to Love daily, they give us commissions in the form of ideas. Instead of using our imaginations, Love wants us to use the Spirit of Love, speaking through our conscience, other people, and life circumstances, to cast a vision to our minds and hearts. The Spirit of Love living in us, after we surrender and commit to Love, has bigger dreams than our imaginations can muster. And the Spirit of Love can make those dreams a reality!

Our Part:

In your dedicated daily time with Love, invite Love to give you ideas for creative service. Then listen to the inner voice of Love for notions of how to serve creatively with your gifts. You may already have a burden or passion to serve some people in unique ways according to your passions. Commit those ideas to Love and then go attempt to do them with the best of your ability. Knock on doors and see what Spirit opens. If Spirit wants it, Love will bless your efforts and it will be a joy, not a chore.

If there is opposition to your efforts to serve creatively, ask Spirit to show you if the opposition is a sign that Love doesn't want you to serve this way, or if the enemies are behind the opposition. Regardless of the answer, remember Love never treats those people opposed to us as the enemies. And neither should we.

Fear, Shame, and Arrogance have many humans they can use as agents of the enemies in our lives. When summoning patience and grace for such agents, it's important to remember we too can be agents of the enemies in other people's lives. There's no place for hypocritical judgement in the Realm of Love. Fighting with such people can suck the joy out of creative service, leave us disillusioned with Love—since we felt led but were thwarted—and wind up hurting our mental health and relationships. Some people have actively or passively set aside daily reconnection with Love due to disillusionment with people or programs they associated with Spirit.

In-fighting amongst funnel gardens of Love is the biggest reason many people don't have any interest in big or small reconnection with Love. When I've presented ideas to people of surrendering and committing to Love, no one has ever said, "Oh, I don't need more Love in my life," or "Don't go pushing Love on me." But when I've asked people why they haven't reconnected with Love, they usually respond with things like, "Those religious people are all hypocrites" or "Religious people are too judgmental." That is a travesty that grieves the Spirit of Love.

Practical

Let's say you were walking down the sidewalk and saw a homeless man with a sign asking for spare change so he can buy some food. If you walked past him and said something like, "You are Loved, have a nice day," but then you didn't put any change in his hat, do you think he's buying your sentiment? No way.

Creative service for those in the Realm of Love must be practical. Love cares about the daily needs of all human beings, whether they're reconnected with Love or not. Love is no respecter of persons. If you are human, the uniqueness of your design and story are what make you immeasurably valuable and lovable to Spirit, and all who are reconnected. Too often I hear complaints like, "Those people who claim to know Spirit are out of step with reality." Thankfully, I see this changing in a lot of Spirit communities. This must be a part of a Love Revolution for the world to take notice. After all, *they will know we're Reconnected with Love...by our love!*

Another hinderance to people reconnecting with Love is the hidden agendas of many funnels of Love. They "love" in order to win people over to Spirit's side. That's not love, that's manipulation. And it's just as easy to perceive as truly loving.

Recently, I was very thirsty and needed some energy so I went to the fridge and retrieved a can of some sugary liquid. As I drank, there was a plastic piece of the label sticking out that jabbed my lips and hurt. Try as I did to remove it, I just couldn't get it off. In disgust I gave up and ditched the can. Sometimes, annoyances prevent us from accessing what we need. Many people are thirsty for Love in their lives. As a representative of the Realm of Love, it's our job not to be annoying plastic pieces of the label. Spirit's agenda is to love. Period. We need to let Spirit oversee the results of loving. Ours is just to focus on creative service that Love inspires in us.

Our Part:

Start your hunt to find practical ways to serve creatively by investigating the needs in your community. You can start by phoning community resource centres, churches, addiction treatment centres, youth drop-in centres, seniors' centres, boys and girls' clubs, hospitals, sports clubs, schools, day-care centres, women's shelters, or homeless shelters—whatever group you have a heart to help. Tell them you want to volunteer your time and talents to help others and ask for their ideas. Before you do this, have a conversation with Love to be led according to Love's plans for your life.

And remember, though we can be agents of Love, we are not Love. We are not the gardeners to other people's gardens. Other funnel gardens are for us to enjoy and appreciate, regardless of the state the garden is in. We can contribute to growth through creative service, but we are not the gardener of their growth! We will notice differences between the various gardens we encounter, but comparison for estimation of quality is not part of the Realm of Love. Love doesn't compare gardens, even though Love *is* the gardener.

Uniqueness

Why is the Mona Lisa priceless? It's probably a combination of being created by a genius and being the only painting created by that person. That's what makes each of us priceless too. We were created by the genius of Love and there's only one of each of us. The uniqueness of our design—as seen in our gifts—and *story*—as seen through our testimonials—are what contributes to the power of Love to transform other funnels into Reconnected gardens.

When I was working with youth in Whitehorse, Yukon territory, I ran youth retreats at a place called Camp Yukon. We'd spend a weekend in the fall and another in the winter gathering teens from all over the north to listen to motivational speakers, sing, dance, and play games. The point was to get them hyped to know and serve Love. And we were quite successful in hyping teens up for the cause of Love. Youth would leave the retreat excited to focus on Spirit and ways to creatively serve Love with their lives, time, and talents.

The problem I noticed was that about a month after each retreat the teens would be back to an apathetic state regarding Spirit. The cares of life, insecurities of growing up, and need for popularity, choked any enthusiasm to stand up for Spirit. I thought we were doing a disservice by hyping without sustaining. So, I sought Love for a way to change this dynamic.

One morning in meditation with Love I received a fresh Revelation to make a difference in the lives of the youth in the north. It was innovative, radical, and absolutely nuts to expect youth to be on board with. That's how I knew it was from Spirit. Love needs me to do the possible. I need Love to do the impossible!

This is what I proposed to my youth group. They were to commit to coming to our youth room every morning before school for an hour of meditation and conversations with Spirit. Three nights a week they were to commit to come back to the youth gathering place for two hours of video and live presentations on the nature and purposes of Love for their lives. At the end of this ten-week training period, they were to commit to two months of summer travel around the Yukon and Alaska doing children and youth camps to share what Spirit had done in their lives. They would put together skits, songs, and presentations to share about Love.

A week after sharing that challenge with the youth group we ran a retreat at Camp Yukon and got kids hyped again to know and serve Love. After the retreat, ten teens signed up for our Spirit training program. During that time Spirit increased those teens' enthusiasm for sharing about Love. They'd go to school every day and strike up conversations with peers about Spirit. They'd bring friends to youth group where they'd be accepted and inspired in ways they never had before. Our youth group went from ten teens to fifty in a few months. A few years later it was at about 150. To my knowledge, 35 years later, it is still going strong, transforming the lives of teens in the north with the Presence and Power of Love.

In the early stages of that movement of Love, one young lady—I'll call her Dee—had been particularly transformed by the power of Love. At thirteen she was sexually abused by several men living in her home. She got pregnant and didn't know who the father was. She gave up that child for adoption. By the time I met her when she was sixteen, she had just been kicked out of school for substance abuse. As you can imagine, her heart and mind were a mess. But Love had a plan for Dee.

I met with Dee every week to help her process and heal the pain of her past. Through the compassion and empathy Spirit stirred in me for this young lady, Love began to transform her life. She became a joyful, vibrant advocate for Spirit as Love healed her mental health, released her from addictive thinking and behaviour, and transformed her relationships.

By the time she graduated from high school, so many teens had been added to the group that most people didn't know her story. They just knew Dee as this outspoken, effervescent advocate for Love. Little did they know, until one day Dee responded to my invitation to share her life story.

As she divulged the details of her past trauma you could hear a pin, and jaws, drop. No one could believe how much pain she'd endured, and yet she'd come through it with such an incredibly beautiful spirit. It was obvious to all that this girl was seriously Reconnected with Love. That night, and for years to come, many people were drawn to Spirit through Dee's story. She became a social worker, had a family, obtained her master's degree, and went on to impact countless lives for Love. Sadly, Dee died in a tragic accident in her 40's. But so many people know Spirit because of her life. And she is now in the presence of the one who IS Love. The uniqueness of our design and stories can be powerfully used by Love to *creatively serve* others in their quest for *mental health* and *relationship* healing.

Our Part:

When you are serving others, being open and vulnerable, when appropriate, is an influential way to inspire growth. Love probably gave us compassion to serve in the first place because Spirit brought us through struggles like those of the ones we help. I can't count how many people have crossed my path to help, who are going through just what I did. Our stories are ammunition in the hands of either the enemies—when we keep them secret—or Love, when we make them known.

Countless clients have told me they were inspired to change, or encouraged others to grow, at a twelve-step meeting where personal stories are shared. In fact, a good deal of the success of those groups lies in the principle of openness and vulnerability. The enemies hate being spoken of openly. They flee when people share how the stories of their lives changed thanks to Love. Perhaps consider if it's appropriate for you to attend that type of group and share openly.

Your unique story of struggle and triumph can influence others to seek Love to change their lives. One person's story can make a huge difference. Unique stories, in the hands of Spirit, change the world. Share your story as much as you can, to whomever needs it and will listen. Make it part of your creative service, and people will be drawn to you and let you influence their growth. In turn, Love will thrill your soul. Making a difference for Spirit is the ride of life.

Power

From the beginning, humankind has sought *power*. Power to rule over others. Power to advance kingdoms and empires. Power to influence nations and attract followers. Power to win contests. But most of those efforts to obtain and exert power have ended in disasters and ruin. The reason is those searching have looked in the wrong places and obtained pseudo-power from the enemies of Love.

Even those reconnected with Love have misunderstood, misrepresented, and misapplied the power of Love. But there have been enough funnels of Love in the past who understood where true power comes from and have written about it in Ancient Revelation. And there have been a few great examples of those endued with the power of Love to keep inspiring us to search and use the power that comes with current revelation.

The Voice of Love is Power. The voice of Love is majestic. Spirit speaks and new life is formed. Love speaks and foes quake. Spirit speaking changes mourning to laughter and sorrow to dancing.

Love's voice brings supernatural healing to mental health and relationships. In fact, it could be argued there is no display of the nature of Love without power. Spirit has spoken, is still speaking, and will keep speaking. All we have to do is listen to the many ways Spirit speaks, to have our creative service infused by the Power of Love.

Love's voice rings through nature. There's a reason our souls are replenished by walking in nature. All creation speaks to Love's powerful aura. Spirit spoke and nature came to be. When we walk, hike, swim, run, drive, paddle, or ride through nature it's as if we're dancing with Love while Spirit whispers to us of our place in creation. Knowing our place brings peace. Abiding in the breath of Love calms the mind and invigorates the soul.

Our Part:

Spend time in nature every week. Think of it as "date time with Love." As you go, invite Spirit to commune with you and speak through nature. When you're out, reflect on all that Love has brought you, taught you, and shown you in your past. Let the air you breathe in become thankfulness as it goes out. Recognize each time in nature as a spiritual moment.

Take time in your nature adventures to listen to Love speak through your conscience about what's next. Invite Spirit to show you the who, what, where, and how of your next creative service. Whenever you're stuck in a rut or just don't know where to go from here, a little time communing with Love in nature will never steer you wrong. It's just easier to hear Spirit outside and get your mind straight. Spend as much time in nature as it takes for Love to refresh, inspire, replenish, and invigorate your vision and desire for creative service. Worship the *creator* of nature, not the *created* nature, lest you give a foothold to the enemies.

Collaborative

The nature of Love's creative service is inclusive and cooperative. When Love inspires a vision in us, we can always be sure of two things: It's too big for us to do alone, and Spirit has most assuredly prepared the hearts and minds of others to join. A body needs all the parts working together to function as it was designed.

When I was asked by a non-profit family-oriented organization to lead their children's department it became clear their programs were antiquated. They hadn't changed the format or curriculum since the 70's. And the organization's board members were mostly farmers over the age of 55. They had no idea there was a need for change, never mind what to do about it.

While discussing the state of the program with volunteers, it became evident I wasn't the only one in whom Spirit had prompted a need for change. It's just that the few who showed the most passion for change had no idea how to go about it. Neither did I really. So, we formed a committee and developed a strategy together. I found myself the youngest of the group, and yet the voice of caution for not changing too much too soon. Never let your age limit Spirit's ability to utilize your enthusiasm and gifts.

We took seven aging farmers to a city three hours' drive away to show them what another organization was accomplishing in kids' programming. They were blown away by the enthusiasm of volunteers and excitement of children to participate in a program that was inspiring and changing kids' lives. After that experience, we had a blank check from the board to make whatever changes we wanted.

We adopted various ideas and materials others in the field were producing and cast a vision to the families in the community for change. The result was going from about twenty tired volunteers to ninety excited new recruits. Participants in the children's department grew by over 300% in the first few months. More leaders were recruited and hired to run the vibrant program. And that children's department is still changing lives twenty years later.

The point is, if Love has put an idea for creative service in our minds, and on our hearts, we're not alone. If Spirit is in it, they will bring others alongside of us to accomplish it. Like trees linked in nature, funnel gardens are connected at the root—the Spirit of Love.

Our Part:

When Love gives you an idea for creative service, pass it by trusted friends you know to be reconnected with Love. One principle in the Realm of Love is there is wisdom in the counsel of many. Getting as much advice from as many trusted sources is crucial for plans to succeed. Love has spoken many creative ideas into the minds and hearts of people that have never come to pass because those people refused to share them with others. Perhaps such people allowed fear to sway them from sharing.

Maybe those people shared their initiatives with those not daily attuned to Love. Some great plans don't become reality because they get shared with doubters, cynics, and criticizers. Remember, when people make a big reconnection with Love, but don't turn their daily attention to Spirit, they can just as easily be agents of the enemies as those disconnected with Love. Know a person's heart before you entrust Love's beautiful creative service ideas to them.

Spirit commissions us to serve creatively by spreading the Truth of Love in the Spirit of Love. Some people we spread Love's truth to will immediately reject it due to being influenced by Fear, Shame, or Arrogance. Love them anyway.

Other people will accept our messages of Love initially. But then they'll stray away from Spirit because they haven't allowed Spirit to fully heal their past. They allow enemy fortresses to remain in their mind and influence their thinking and attitudes. So, the enemies gradually choke Love out of them. Love them anyway.

Still others will gladly receive Love through our creative service in a superficial way. But then the cares, worries and busyness of life drown out the voice of Spirit. They never fully reconnect with Love, so they never mature in Spirit. Love them anyway.

When we don't daily reconnect with Love, it's easy for creative service to dry up. When we take our eyes off Spirit or entertain ourselves with that which is contrary to Spirit's heart for us, we lose sight of the reason for creative service. In that case, we start to take our cues from people rather than Love. We look to people for validation for creative service and inevitably get disappointed and discouraged, as not everyone will validate our service.

When that happens, we may stay within Spirit communities, but it will only be for show. We settle for the appearance of Love rather than pressing in for the power of Love. Yet no one is drawn to the form of Love without the vibrancy of Love. So our complacency and boredom within such groups neither fulfills us nor attracts anyone else. It's just like we're in a Spirit club that people can take or leave. And many leave...or fall asleep.

The bigger tragedy is that so many struggling with problems in their Mental Health and Relationships turn to the enemies' fake solutions to fix the real problem. The enemies promote ancient counterfeit philosophies by repackaging and rebranding them. Modern masses, disillusioned by a fraudulent version of the Realm of Love and clogged up funnels of Love, flock to these "new" ideas for hope and transformation. The Spirit of Love is left grieved and quenched. And no lasting changes are realized by the duped masses.

But the Spirit of Love is never thwarted. Spirit is always at work to awaken agents to arise and act. If Spirit has been speaking to you lately and bringing about energy and excitement to your soul, then it means a new chapter is about to unfold.

A new commission is being issued by Love. The calling is to delight ourselves in Love. Tune out the world, focus attention and give all our time to Spirit. Those who hang with Spirit all the time glow inside and that radiates through our energy pours. When Love's light is placed in us it turns to creative service. Such service draws others to Spirit, and they are inspired to seek Love for healing, wholeness, and purpose. It is Spirit's plan to recruit, heal, commission, and utilize more funnel gardens of Love. Get in on the plan!

Chapter 11: Love Increases Enduring Integrity

One of the ways Spirit designed us to hear the Spirit of Love is through our *conscience*. It is about far more than just knowing right from wrong. Our conscience can be seen as Love's smartphone inside us. It has many useful *Apps*.

There's Conscience Apps for scheduling, weather, sports, news, health, banking, translation, spiritual vitality, and many more. Everything Love wants to tell us can come through our clear conscience.

But if the battery is dead, our conscience isn't fully and daily reconnected with Love, or if there's a virus—as when our conscience is influenced by the enemies—then we may not hear Spirit. We may be misled by what we think is Love but isn't, or we'll become disheartened in our efforts to be blessed by Spirit. That can make us even worse off than if we never reconnected with Love in the first place. See how important our conscience is? It's essential to let Love clean our conscience so we can use all the apps. But after it's cleaned, exploring the Realm of Love through conscience apps becomes an exciting inner adventure!

I've read about a man who had the clearest conscience of any human that ever lived. He lived a long time ago before social media, news media, and Hollywood existed, so things happened in his life we might not be able to relate to. However, since he's the best example there is, I'm going to use his life as an example of how to use conscience apps. And I'm going to put old stories into modern context so it's easier for you to relate. Please allow me the creative leeway. I'll call this man Joshua. Josh for short.

Weather App

This App is about knowing the spiritual temperature of a group of people. We call it "reading the room." One time, Josh was approached at a party by a group of thugs who told him they'd found his sister in bed with a man who wasn't her husband. These hoodlums were trying to mock Josh because they hated what they perceived as his "goody-two-shoes" ways. His purity of Love triggered Shame's lies to them that they weren't enough.

Without saying a word, Josh picked up a piece of paper and started writing. He wrote each of their names and beside it a detail of something awful each of them had done in the recent past. When he completed the list in their view, he looked up and said, "Anyone who's never done anything bad, feel free to condemn my sister." As each man saw his name on the list, the group left the party one by one. Josh's clean conscience allowed him to know the group's spiritual temperature.

Not too long ago I met a man who said he was so spiritually in tune with Love that he could enter a room full of people and instantly know everyone in the room's predominant struggles. Whether it was addictions, hatred, jealousy, anxiety, depression, or envy, he could tell intuitively what areas each person was dealing with. I knew his integrity well enough to believe him.

Love gives such spiritual insight for other people's benefit. In the case of Josh, Spirit was protecting a woman who was being attacked by Shame, as well as highlighting for bullies that they needed to go deal with their own issues rather than judge someone else. In the case of my friend, it was so that he could give more insightful counsel from Love to release clogged-up funnels. When we have a clear conscience, Love can let us sense the spiritual temperature of others to creatively serve them.

News App

This App is how Love lets some people know what is secretly happening or about to happen. In the movie, "What Women Want" the main character is suddenly endued with the ability to read women's minds. He uses his temporary power to manipulate and coerce for selfish gain. But this ability has been given in real life in the past and present.

On numerous occasions, Josh knew what people were thinking and addressed their thoughts without having to ask them. Usually, their thoughts were complaining accusations against him, instigated by Fear and Pride. Yet Josh took the opportunity to expose people's thoughts for useful lessons from Love.

At other times, Josh shared information that had not yet happened, but eventually did. A clear conscience allowed Love to show him the future. One time a friend of Josh's was bragging about his loyalty to Josh and how much strength of character he'd formed through Josh's teachings. Josh reacted to his companion's bragging by telling him, "In a very short time you're going to abandon me and deny you ever knew me." Josh did this for his buddy's own good. He was assuring him that even though he knew the betrayal was coming, he loved his friend and would welcome him back when he was ready. That's what Love does through a clear conscience: it sees the future and gives grace that changes lives.

Sports App

A clear conscience enables us to identify who the real opposition of Love is. Those disconnected from Spirit are not the enemies of Love. The current and future funnel gardens of Love are not the real enemies either. It's only through a clear conscience that we can maintain that distinction and treat the agents of Fear,

Shame, and Arrogance with honour, even while they're being used by the enemies to attack us.

There were many occasions when Josh encountered people who were so affected by the enemies that they exhibited physical traits of evil. Josh's clear conscience let Love show him exactly what was going on inside such people. Then Love gave Josh's clear conscience a plan as to how to set such people free from the enemies. So supernatural was the restoration to sanity of these folks that their transformation after an encounter with Josh led them to dedicate their lives to promote Josh and his teachings to others.

In my own life I have seen people instantly restored to sanity after years of being afflicted by the enemies. On several occasions, at the request of myself or those I was with, Spirit demonstrated great power to completely free people of their addictive desires and behaviour. Others were instantly freed from anxiety and depression, with no future symptoms. Spirit won these contests for people's minds through funnel gardens who had a clear conscience.

Health App

I have witnessed and heard credible reports of blind people receiving their sight, deaf people hearing, and lame people walking. Even the idea that this could be possible today came from studying the life of Josh. Spirit cured a lot of sick people because of Josh's clear conscience and obedience to use it for Love.

Scheduling, Banking, Spiritual Apps and More

Spirit can use our clear conscience to let us know when we're supposed to do or say things for Love. They can utilize our clear conscience to give money and resources to those who need them. They can also increase our bank account for our needs and those Love wants to bless through us. Love also shows us spiritual mysteries previously hidden for us to discover. There are countless conscience Apps they can give us.

Josh's clear conscience was a unique prototype. There will never be another Josh. However, though Josh has disappeared in this physical world, the Spirit of Josh lives on. That's the Spirit of Truth in Love's Realm that's used to clear our Conscience when we surrender to Love.

We can have a clear conscience like Josh's through big and daily surrenders. After Love clears our conscience all the apps are at our disposal. We can become like Josh. We can see the future, know what's going on in secret, and display great power to heal others. But it's all about staying connected with Love through surrender.

Love deserves all the attention and affirmation from us and everyone else who utilizes conscience Apps. And the praise of Spirit is what spurs on greater power within the Apps. Our mental health and relationships are revitalized as we attune our daily attention to Love. Our desires to serve Spirit creatively are replenished as we take the greatest pleasure in Love.

It is no wonder the enemies continually attempt to distract us from Love and our conscience Apps. The enemies usually do this through the busyness of the good that distracts us from the great. The enemies also use comparative complaints, critical judgements, and fake solutions that have the appearance of usefulness but lack the real power of Love.

Most of all, the enemies try to dirty our conscience through bitterness, lust, and deception. These come through lies, doubts, worries, and temptations. We sometimes trade peace, calm, and purity for the allure of quick pleasure. Then when we come to our senses, Fear and Shame are right there to bring our thoughts down. What do we do to get rid of such thoughts? Right back to the quick pleasures that tore us away from serenity. And so, the cycle of death can even affect the conscience of the surrendered.

Guard your conscience. Take it through Love's carwash called big surrender and then keep it shiny with a cloth called daily surrender. The payoff is endless powerful conscience Apps for supernatural mental health and relationships!

Our Part:

The first step to clearing our conscience is obviously surrender to Spirit. Spirit is the one who clears the conscience. We can't clean it alone after it's been tainted. A clear conscience is a grace gift from Love. If you haven't already had that conversation with Spirit, have it now. Tell Spirit all the things you can remember doing, saying, or thinking that weren't in line with Love. Then ask Spirit to clear your conscience through forgiveness. Ask for forgiveness and give yourself forgiveness too. That's how you delete Shame's viruses in you.

After that conversation, do a creative exercise. Think of your funeral—an event that is hopefully many, many years from now. Imagine a family member, friend, and coworker getting up and talking about you. What good things would you want them to be able to truthfully say about you? What would you want them to say about your character, mind, heart, relationships, and traits they noticed. Write their speeches for them accordingly.

After you've written those funeral talks, analyze the speeches to uncover what they say about your values. Pull out key value-words expressed or implied in your imagined remembrances. How you wish to be remembered says what you truly esteem for your life. If you want to be remembered as a funny person, clearly you value levity and comradery. If you want people to say you inspired them to grow, that shows you value meaningful influence. Maybe you want people to say they could always trust what you said to be accurate and wise. That says you value honesty and wisdom.

After you've pulled out as many value-words as possible, ask yourself if that's how you're living now. Maybe some ways you behave, relate, or communicate need to be altered to line up with your ideals. You could even ask someone who cares about you that will give you honest feedback if your speeches ring true today. Summon humility to press past flattering niceties and get to the heart of what needs to change about you so that your conscience can stay pure.

It's your conscience, informed by Love, that will let you know how to keep it clear. After my conscience was cleared, little things I'd previously glossed over started gnawing at me. I'd receive an overheard judgmental remark with typical derision and then a few minutes later my conscience would tell me that wasn't in line with the Love I'm reconnected with. So, the next week I'd resolve to fix that and then notice my criticalness towards a presentation being given. And again, the newly cleared conscience would clear its proverbial throat. But before you think this dynamic annoying, my cleared conscience also bore joyful fruit.

Having a cleared conscience led me to make amends to all kinds of people I'd wronged in behaviour, attitudes, and words. The feeling of making amends was so liberating I just wanted to find anyone and everyone that could possibly have something against me and give them a verbal hug.

Then I noticed the people I'd made amends with began to treat me differently. One person started humming and singing in my presence for the first time in over thirty years. Other people were more open and vulnerable with me. Some people apologized to me for wrongs I hadn't even noticed they had committed.

After that, Spirit started leading people to me that needed my conscience Apps. A girl I was sharing with was having a particularly difficult time releasing her pain and Love reminded me of an old poem I'd long forgotten about. When I pulled it up online, she read it and started crying and her anxiety was released in that moment.

An old colleague phoned me up and invited me to collaborate on an exciting project that could lead to changing many people's lives, including my own. Love then prompted me to forgive a group of people who'd really hurt me in the past. Within the confines of a clear conscience, it took only a few minutes for Spirit to convince me to rejoin that group I'd been bitter towards.

The point is, Love flows through a clear conscience. Let Spirit clear it through surrender, and then guard it with all your mind, heart, and strength. But if you go against it, rest assured, Love has the most powerful tool to re-clear it.

SECTION FIVE: The Power Tools of Love

Chapter 12: Grace

Mercy and *Grace* are not the same. When we do something bad, and know we deserve something bad back, getting *mercy* is good. Getting grace is way better though. The difference between mercy and grace is like the difference between a *million* dollars and a *billion* dollars. Let me illustrate the contrast with an analogy.

Let's say you were on death row because you committed a heinous crime. Even if you were incredibly remorseful and genuinely vowed to change your ways, you know inside you deserve to die. That's justice. When the conscience is functioning according to its design, if it doesn't stop us from doing wrong, it certainly lets us know what we deserve for the wrong.

But let's say during your trial the judge sensed you were genuinely sorry for your crime and was confident you would never do that again. Nevertheless, that judge had to dole out justice according to the law. Thus, your status on death row awaiting your penalty. If that judge commuted your sentence to life in prison, instead of execution by electric chair, that's mercy. And I'm sure you would be quite thankful. Getting mercy when we deserve justice makes us glad.

But let's say instead of the judge mercifully commuting your sentence, that judge comes to visit you on death row one day. The judge reminds you of your crime and what you deserve, and you don't deny it at all. The judge tells you it wouldn't be right for someone not to pay for your crime, as you are sentenced to do. You agree again, wholeheartedly. Then the judge takes off his robe and informs you *he* is going to take your place. *He is going to die on your behalf*, and you can walk out of prison a free person. *That's grace!*

But wait, there's even more to grace. When you get out of prison you discover the judge has arranged for you to inherit and live in *His* house! You get *His* car, *His* bank account, and *His* clothes. Then you find out *His* family members want to get to know you. They heard their father talk about you, what great potential you have and how valuable and lovable their father found you to be. When you get together, they are so incredibly kind and generous to you. *That's grace!*

But wait, there's even more to grace. Then the family informs you that the judge made arrangements for you to study to become whatever you want in life. The best educators in the country have been put on retainer to teach and train you in the areas you're gifted and passionate about. You get a fresh start, with unlimited resources at your disposal, to make the most of the new life you've been afforded. All because of *grace*.

See the difference between mercy and grace? Mercy is good. Grace is lavish. Mercy leads to thankfulness. Grace leads to transformation. Are you telling me you wouldn't be passionately motivated to show your gratefulness for grace? When we truly know what the bad parts of us deserve, and we truly understand the nature of grace, it motivates us to serve, give, and live with passionate love for the one who took our place!

Grace is the gate to the Realm of Love. There's no entrance to the Realm without it. Grace is the greatest swap meet in the Realm of Love. We give our bad at the gate and in return get good. In fact, we end up as co-owners of the Realm. It's by grace we receive the Spirit and mind of Love. And that mind is sound—peaceful, calm, and stable with security and significance. Why wouldn't it be sound? It has access to all the wisdom and riches of the Realm of Love. Let's take a closer look at all Love does in our lives through grace.

Grace Gives Its Recipients Authority of the Realm of Love

Anyone can love people who love them first or love them back. But grace empowers us to love with no return. Receiving grace emboldens us to love those who can't, or won't, love us back. In this we give what Love gave us. That marks us as members of the Realm of Love.

Police officers show their identity and have authority because of the badge they carry. Grace is Love's badge. If we funnel gardens don't show it to outsiders, or insiders, no one recognizes our authority. Then they won't let us speak into their lives the Truth of Love that can transform them as we're being transformed. In fact, without the badge of grace, why would anyone want to let us creatively serve them? Without grace, creative service is sterile—it might be pleasing in the moment, but there's no power to create life.

Love also uses grace to empower us to resist the enemies. This is how it works...

Grace so thrills our hearts and minds that we just can't shut up about how great Love is and all that they do for us. Speaking the truth of Love to ourselves and others focuses our minds and hearts on Love. The enemies hate that and stay away. They have no space to attack a mind that's constantly focused on and spouting out Love. The enemies can't stand the openness and vulnerability that the grace of Love inspires in growing funnel gardens. The sacrifices Spirit made on our behalf, and our spoken stories, defeat our enemies.

Grace Gives Its Recipients Lasting Motivation to Change and Serve

Remember when you were on death row a few paragraphs ago? Well now imagine that same judge approaching a person walking down the street and announcing to them he was going to take their place and die for them. It probably wouldn't get the same reaction as an inmate on death row, right? It would probably get a weird look or mockery of what they'd perceive to be some escaped psych patient disrobing and spouting delusions.

If you don't know you're being affected by the enemies—Fear, Shame, and Arrogance—someone telling you Love can free you won't arouse a big response. But when you know you're being attacked, and when you know you can't break free of the enemies on your own, being set free has a profound impact. When someone in that state receives the grace of Love, it not only powerfully changes them, but it also makes them willing to do anything for Spirit, for the rest of their lives.

That's why two thousand years after Josh lived and died (OK his real name is Jesus if you haven't figured that out yet) people are still following and doing things for him. Grace makes us so thankful that we'd do anything for the one who IS Love that gave it to us. It's because we freely receive the unconditional acceptance and favour of Love that we surrender.

We don't surrender to earn acceptance and favour. That's self-righteousness, and that breeds critical judgment, selfish ambition, and vain conceit. Trying to earn the riches of Love and the Realm is like trying to get to Paris, France by driving around a cul-de-sac in Paris, Texas. Different places, different routes, and completely different means to get there. People trying to earn the grace of Love get burnt out and repel others from Love. There's no life or power in self-righteousness. It's another fake solution to a real problem sponsored by our enemies. It falls under the category of control.

I've seen people really set free by Spirit using grace to make them the best versions of themselves. Their fervour to serve Love is infectious. Their impact on the Realm of Love is powerful. People with mental health and relationship problems are drawn to them and changed just from hanging out with such folks. That kind of influence is available to all of us funnel gardens who surrender in big and daily ways.

Grace Gives Its Recipients the Comradery and Comfort of Family

When I served as a counsellor at a residential treatment centre for addictions, there were many clients who returned. Some needed further treatment after relapsing, others were just visiting to tell us about their new lives. The difference usually involved who they hung around with after treatment was over. Returning clients almost always went right back to the same social group that influenced their continued addictions. Visitors often told me no one in their new social circle uses substances. Who knew my dad was right...Show me your friends and I'll tell you who you are.

When we surrender to Spirit in big and daily ways, Love resides in us. But for true unity, and the power that comes from that, we need to reside in Love. That's where Love's funnel gardens become funnel garden residents. When Love brings us into the Realm, all the other funnel gardens of Love become our family.

The grace of Love makes us thrilled to be together with others who've been set free from the enemies. We get to hear other people's stories of struggle and triumph. We get to discover all the mysteries and highlight all the attributes of Love who changed us. And as we hang out, we get to see what Love sees in everybody adopted into Love's family. The comradery and comfort of family soothes, calms, and nurtures our invigorated mental health and relationships. Spirit communities also strengthen our faith, as we realize we're not alone in our surrendered state.

Grace Gives Its Recipients the Power to Impart Grace

Here's how we know if grace is being used by us and other funnel garden residents. Remember the story we looked at about the servant who was forgiven a million dollars? He went out and was a demanding jerk to his own servant. That's a clear sign that grace was not received. When grace isn't being used to manage relationships with others, something is amiss in Reconnection with Love.

There is NO reconnection with Love happening where grace is not present. Remember, grace is receiving and giving undeserved favour. If we're giving people what they deserve—good or bad—that's not grace.

I once had a pastor friend who was a mentor in my life. He took me under his wing when I was a young snot-nosed college grad. He taught me a lot about how to lead and help people. He even conducted my wedding ceremony. But, sixteen years later, when I initiated divorce with my wife, that pastor friend told me he would now have nothing to do with me. I'm sure he thought he was doing the right thing. I'm sure he was giving me what I deserved. He just wasn't giving me grace.

A few months after my divorce, I was getting my transmission fixed and I discovered the guy who owned the shop used to be a pastor. When he found out I had just been through a divorce and lost all my Christian friends—who had abandoned me, thinking that's what I deserved—this stranger told me he wanted to help me through my hard time. He knew two other men who were going through a divorce, and he suggested we all get together for breakfast to support one another. That turned into a weekly event that brought me great comfort and hope. Love replaced deserved with grace. That changed my life. That's the sign grace is present. Grace empowers recipients to change people's lives.

Chapter 13: Thankfulness

I know of no greater tool to place in the hands of Love than thankfulness. Grace is generated by our Spirit; thankfulness is generated by us. Grace is given by Love to draw us, and those we share it with, into a closer relationship with the Spirit of Love. Thankfulness is how we partner with the Spirit to transform our mental health and relationships. Grace is Jesus hitting it out of the park. Thankfulness is us running the bases.

Thankfulness is not optional. It is to our mental health what the gas pedal is to our cars. We can't move towards healthy living and relating without thankfulness. It's vital because it relates to so many other essential elements of healthy living. Thankfulness is the hub around which every other crucial component of supernatural mental health and relationships revolves. So, let's take a look at how thankfulness relates to humility, hope, perspective/attitude, love, faith, emotions, grace, and forgiveness.

Thankfulness and Humility

One of my favourite sitcoms is *The Big Bang Theory*. I love the idea of someone having a mind that retains all the information given to them. Perhaps it's because I wish that were me. Regardless, even Sheldon Cooper had to have people tell/show/teach him what he knows. And that's the truth for all of us.

No matter what nature we're born with, we all need others to teach us what we need to know and do to have a great life. We all need mentors to demonstrate for us how to live a peaceful, joyful, loving life. No one comes into this world with full knowledge of how to live. Even Jesus had to learn submission to authority.

Thankfulness promotes humility because in it we are acknowledging our need for others. As we practice gratitude, we are giving honour to those who went before us to glean the information given to us. We are showing respect to those who helped us become what we are. Practicing thankfulness daily is a great way to put on humility like a coat. It prepares us for whatever conditions we encounter each day.

Thankfulness and Hope

Hope is helped by precedent. What I mean is, if you can see something good happened in the past, it increases your confidence that it can happen in the future too. Thankfulness is proclaiming a spiritual legal precedent that tells the enemies to get their tentacles off our hopes. Thankfulness highlights the good that has happened in the past. That consistent practice increases hope. And, what good are hopes if you can't get them up?

Love wants to place more and more hope in our hearts. Hope in the heart sooths worry in the mind. We can partner with Spirit in this desire by completing the design. The missing piece in the design, and our part in co-creating, is our thankful words and attitude.

Thankfulness and Perspective/Attitude

What I mean by good is bad too. That's an odd statement, isn't it? Let me explain. There's an old saying that starts, "Consider it pure joy when you face trials of many kinds…" But the saying concludes "…because you know the testing of your life leads to perseverance, and perseverance leads to character." Bad can be made into good, depending on how you view it.

Since the Spirit of Love gives free will, Spirit must allow bad things to happen to "good" people. So, Love turns the bad we experience into good. Like fertilizer to a tree, the bad we experience produces growth. To negate grudges, resentments, and bitterness from springing up and derailing our faith and mental health, Love provides us with a tool to keep us focused on Spirit's righteous intent. That tool is thankfulness.

Thankfulness in the face of undesired circumstances changes "not enough" into "more than enough." When we are thankful as we go through the storms of life, we are keeping our eyes on what the trial is producing at the end. Suffering builds strength. When I go to the gym and want to gain strength, I don't lift easy weights. To grow strong, I need to lift hard weights. The same can be said of the soul. To grow a strong soul—to become emotionally mature—we must go through difficult times. Being thankful amid those hard times helps us maintain Love's perspective. If we maintain Love's perspective, we can forge a positive mental attitude regardless of our experienced circumstances.

Thankfulness and Love

Thankfulness is like spiritual glue. Whatever we're most thankful for is what we will have the most admiration and respect for. Those qualities lead to loyalty. My dad is my best friend and the man I most admire in this world. I thank Spirit every day for putting me in his family and giving me such a great manager, mentor, and trusted confidant. My thankfulness for that man in my life strengthens the energy of my commitment to be and do whatever my dad needs.

Thankfulness is a spark plug to the engine of Love. If I'm most thankful for the red mustang sitting in my driveway (relax, I'm just dreaming), I'm likely to spend a lot of time and energy polishing and protecting it. Whatever we're most thankful for is what we'll value the most. That value carries action. That action is the sign of love. Thankfulness leads to action, which is the "tell" of love.

Hollywood seems to promote the idea that if we don't feel love then we should get out of a relationship so we're happier. Love promotes the idea that if we don't feel love, start acting lovingly until your feelings of love increase. One practical way we can kickstart the feelings of love we all crave is to be thankful for that which we want to increase love towards. In essence, if you want to increase your loving feelings towards someone, start articulating your thankfulness more frequently. The more the thankfulness, the more the Spirit of Love flows through those surrendered to the one who is Love.

Thankfulness and Faith

The idea of history comes into play again here. Our history, and the history of Love. If we spend time regularly thinking back over our lives and thanking the one who is Love for all the good and bad memories, we are left with two conclusions.

First, we're going to see that there is a planner that has designed and carried out a plan for our good. The blessings and lessons are intended to grow us into the best versions of ourselves. And they will if we let them and look to Spirit for insights and healing.

Second, we're going to have assurance that the one who began a good work in us will complete it. So, there's good things ahead. This increases faith. As we read about how Love blessed and taught others through world history, we can get the same kind of assurance. Thankfulness increases our awareness that we're not alone and Love isn't finished with us yet. Thankfulness for the past gives us boldness to step out in faith for the future.

Thankfulness and Emotions

As we've seen, feelings are messengers from the soul to let us know if our needs are being met. When we inject emotions with thankfulness it's like steroids to the good ones and virus protection to the bad ones. When we feel content, adding thankfulness makes us even more content. That seems like a "duh, no kidding" moment, so I'll let it be. But on the other hand, when we feel sorrow, adding thankfulness alters what we're looking for. Just the idea that it's possible to add thankfulness to sadness or anger or grief may seem strange at first. Until we realize that Love designed a system where we grow into better versions of ourselves through suffering. In that light, thankfulness appears more plausible. And it changes our expectations in times of trials. When we're thankful during the storms, we're keeping our eyes on the big picture of what Love is doing in us that is good during this difficult chapter. So, thankfulness wards off despair during times of trouble, which keeps fear and shame at bay. Thus, thankfulness is virus protection to the soul when we combine it with any emotional experience.

Thankfulness and Grace

As I've already noted, grace means experiencing good when bad is deserved. And grace has a lot of powerful effects on a person, including loyalty and service to the one giving the grace. What we must note here is that thankfulness before and after grace is an essential component to its power.

Thankfulness promotes humility. That's the mechanism that shows us our need for grace. We must acknowledge we need grace for us to be willing to receive it. Thankful thoughts till the ground of the heart to prepare it for grace. Thankful hearts are humble hearts that are actively resisting the pride that negates the power of grace.

After grace has been received, sometimes the danger is to use it as a license to do whatever we want, including judging others or becoming callous to the Spirit of Love. But maintaining an attitude and habit of thankfulness prevents spiritual pride from setting in. Thankfulness keeps our hearts soft, which is a perfect state for receiving more and more grace and peace. Thankfulness and true grace are inseparable.

Thankfulness and Forgiveness

Finally, we say thank you to the creator by living as we should. Following our conscience that wants to love others with integrity is the biggest thank you we can give the one who is Love. By implication, that means any time we go against our conscience—any time we are unloving in speech, attitude, and action—we are saying the opposite of thank you to our designer. I believe that's something like "screw you." Not something you want to say to the Almighty Love of the universe. But we all do it at various times. No one is perfect. So, another way we say thank you to Love is by saying sorry, both to Love and those with skin on that we hurt. Making amends is a powerful way to restore a joyful loving heart.

As you can see, thankfulness is a useful partner to every element of healthy living. We need to practice thankfulness in order to initiate and maintain positive mental health and relationships. And, if it isn't apparent already, let me state the obvious: to be effective, thankfulness needs to be directed to the Spirit who is responsible for all good things in our lives.

Thankfulness is our way of pleasing our maker. And I don't mean "pleasing" in a gaining approval way. I mean it in a "dad has just taught his child how to play soccer and now he's watched him score his first goal" type of way. It gives our Spirit great joy seeing us function as we were meant to. Love is always paying attention to us like proud parents. Thankfulness is our way of paying more attention to them.

But how do we express thankfulness? I'm thankful you asked. Well, words are the easy part. And they're not always easy for everyone. Saying thank you is an act of humility, as we've seen. That's a challenge for the arrogant, the fiercely independent, and the stubborn. It's also a challenge for the hurting and bitter among us.

Many people with mental health issues and a history of being abused, abandoned, or neglected in relationships would ask what on earth they have to be thankful for. On the surface, who could blame them? If this life is about prosperity and happiness, then no, those folks don't have much to be thankful for. But maybe life isn't about those things. Maybe that's a lie to get people pursuing and prioritizing the wrong thing, so the right thing is left neglected.

As we've discussed in this book, life is about reconnecting with Love in a big, and daily, way. Life is about growing and flowing with Love. Love doesn't plan our pain. Nor does the Spirit take away other's ability to inflict it, for that's not the nature of Love. Spirit uses pain to bring beauty, as we allow. With this view, there's always a reason to be thankful. Saying thank you for our pleasure AND our pain is a great path to a lighter soul.

But thankfulness isn't just verbal. Gratitude is an attitude. As such, we can show thankfulness with our actions and reactions. Imagine someone cutting you off in traffic while you maintain an attitude of thankfulness for owning a car and being able to drive to work rather than walk. Wouldn't that change your reaction versus having an attitude of entitlement in that scenario? Or how about focusing on your gratitude for the time spent with a loved one in the face of their demise. Not easy, I'm sure. But if it's humanly possible then you should imagine you're capable of doing it. Living a thankful life is possible with consistent practice. And it's not optional. It's essential to developing and maintaining positive mental health and relationships.

Final Thoughts on Reconnecting with Love

Reconnecting with Love is essential for life. Reconnecting with Love is not a quaint optional idea. It's not a whimsical literary fantasy. There is no life without Love. And there's no getting to Love without Truth. And the truth is, our need to reconnect with Love in one big way, and daily ways, is the *only* way to build supernatural mental health and relationships. It's the *only* way to get our needs met. It's the *only* way to defeat our enemies—Fear, Shame, and Arrogance. It's the *only* way to creatively serve to make a lasting impact on the lives of others. And it's the *only* way to access the power of grace.

The one who IS Love is unique. Love is a parent, a protector, a provider, and a friend. Love is a king, a superhero, and a warrior. Love is a deliverer, redeemer, and confidant. Love is a leader, a healer, and a refuge.

Love is the only one who changes lives. Love wants to push out the worst in us. Love wants to get rid of the enemies' influence in our minds and hearts. Love hates when we're attacked, confused, and disconnected. Love wants to restore and unite relationships. Love gives us a good reputation, hidden riches, and easy paths. And Love is someone to be most thankful for.

Love designed us to be wonderfully weird, goofy, strange, and different. Love wants to draw out the best in us. Love is always for our authentic selves. Love accepts us unconditionally and helps us connect with other funnel gardens. Love improves our character, leads us to integrity, and promotes our reputation.

Love never judges or criticizes. Love never puts us down or shames us. Love never rejects or condemns us. And Love chastises the people who do that to us, but in really gentle ways to help them realize their mistakes so they can change too. In the end, Love gives us choices and freedom.

Why would you NOT want to Reconnect with Love?

Love does *BIG* things in quiet ways. By that I mean Love uses a lot of little things to accomplish a lot of little changes in a person's life. Over the course of time, all those little changes make a big difference. Spirit is really patient. If you want to partner with Spirit in doing big things, then make the most of the little things to make little changes in your life and the lives of others. The little things are called *Today*! Use this one to *Reconnect with Love*.

Acknowledgements

Though I don't know him personally, Bill Johnson has been influential in my thinking and writing lately. I'd like to thank him for hearing from Love and sharing the Truth of Love. I'd also like to thank Brené Brown for her research and writing regarding shame.

About the Author

Mac (Dean) McMillan is a clinical counsellor who specializes in mental health, addictions, and relationship issues. He has been a practicing therapist for over 35 years, with fourteen years of those spent working with youth who suffered abuse or experienced depression and anxiety. Mac has studied and utilized various therapeutic modalities, such as Cognitive Behavioural Therapy (CBT), Narrative Therapy, Emotional Focused Therapy (EFT), Solution Focused Therapy, Dialectic Behavioural Therapy (DBT), Motivational Interviewing, and Pastoral Counselling. He received his Master of Divinity, with a major in Marriage and Family Counselling, from Briercrest Seminary in Caronport, Saskatchewan.

Mac has a private practice in West Kelowna, British Columbia. He does online counselling as well as in-person counselling. Having resided in three countries, several provinces, and two territories, Mac has encouraged and inspired people from all age groups and walks of life. He lived in China for five years and helped people learn English and taught them life skills. He also lived in Thailand for a year, where he facilitated small group workshops at an international wellness centre. Mac has worked with the Inuit people and has a special place in his heart for those who have suffered greatly. He has also had many clients from the LGBTQ community, who have experienced anxiety, depression, abuse, and trauma. Mac has also done extensive public speaking in churches, high schools, and colleges. He has developed and delivered presentations on mental health and spiritual topics for audiences of over 300 people, on three different continents. He even taught a public speaking course for a semester at a university in Thailand!

Mac has three daughters and four grandchildren. In his spare time, he enjoys golfing and paddleboarding. He is also an active member of a faith community. He can be reached for counselling sessions, or booked for speaking engagements, at macmcmillan0310@gmail.com.

www.ingramcontent.com/pod-product-compliance
Lightning Source LLC
LaVergne TN
LVHW022220200926
848481LV00006B/2043